All Things Georgian

Dedicated to
Luke & Aeron

All Things Georgian

Tales from the Long Eighteenth-Century

Joanne Major and Sarah Murden

PEN & SWORD HISTORY

First published in Great Britain in 2019 by
Pen & Sword History
An imprint of
Pen & Sword Books Ltd
Yorkshire – Philadelphia

HB ISBN 978 1 52674 461 6
PB ISBN 978 1 52675 785 2

A CIP catalogue record for this book is
available from the British Library.

Printed and bound in India by Replika Press Pvt. Ltd.

Pen & Sword Books Limited incorporates the imprints of Atlas,
Archaeology, Aviation, Discovery, Family History, Fiction, History,
Maritime, Military, Military Classics, Politics, Select, Transport, True
Crime, Air World, Frontline Publishing, Leo Cooper, Remember When,
Seaforth Publishing, The Praetorian Press, Wharncliffe Local History,
Wharncliffe Transport, Wharncliffe True Crime and White Owl.

For a complete list of Pen & Sword titles please contact

PEN & SWORD BOOKS LIMITED
47 Church Street, Barnsley, South Yorkshire, S70 2AS, England
E-mail: enquiries@pen-and-sword.co.uk
Website: www.pen-and-sword.co.uk

Or

PEN AND SWORD BOOKS
1950 Lawrence Rd, Havertown, PA 19083, USA
E-mail: Uspen-and-sword@casematepublishers.com
Website: www.penandswordbooks.com

Contents

Acknowledgements

We would like to thank Retford Town Hall, Bassetlaw District Council, the Garrick Club, Aberystwyth University School of Art Museum and Galleries, the Rijksmuseum and the Philadelphia Museum of Art for allowing us to use paintings from their collections. Also Northumberland Archives who supplied a key piece of information that helped to identify one of the people mentioned within these pages.

As always, we would like to thank the whole team at Pen & Sword Books for their continued support and belief in us.

Joanne Major and Sarah Murden
2019

Introduction

What was the 'long eighteenth-century' and what made it so special?

The 'long eighteenth-century' is a term often used to loosely describe the historical period from the late seventeenth-century up to the death of George IV in 1830. When writing this compendium of true stories, we have defined it as the period just prior to the turn of the century through to the death of George IV in 1830.

It was a period of great change with many long-running battles between countries: think Jacobite rebellions, the American Revolutionary War and the Battle of Waterloo, and also conflicts between the social classes, with the French Revolution resulting in many of the elite losing their heads courtesy of 'Madame Guillotine'. In Britain too, people rose up against chronic famine and unemployment and there was a growing radicalism on these shores. However, technological advances and the Industrial Revolution were to transform Britain. In the second half of the eighteenth-century Britain became a world leader in the mechanization of tasks, moving from hand-powered work and the cottage industry of frame-work knitters to the invention of the loom and large-scale mills and factories.

Huge leaps in the advancement of science and exploration were made during the era. Within this book you can read about the astronomical discoveries of the Herschels and – perhaps – gain a different perspective on the renowned naturalist and botanist Sir Joseph Banks who, with the explorer Captain Cook, discovered new lands and advanced our scientific knowledge of the natural world.

The first balloon flight and the introduction of a vaccine for smallpox were among the many varied achievements of the era which ended with the introduction of the railway to Britain.

The Hanoverians

On 1 August 1714, the 54-year-old George, Elector of Hanover ascended the thrones of Britain and Ireland to become King George I, heralding the start of the Hanoverian dynasty in this country which would see three of his descendants take the crown successively as George II, III and IV (and finally George IV's brother,

William, whose seven-year reign bridged the gap between the Georgian and Victorian eras).

The reigning Stuart dynasty had come to an end with the death of Queen Anne who, despite seventeen pregnancies, had no surviving heirs and George, as the great-grandson of James I, was the choice of those who wanted a king of the Protestant religion. The 'Old Pretender', Queen Anne's Catholic half-brother, James Francis Edward Stuart, challenged King George's right to reign. In Britain support for the new king was mixed: by and large, the Whig politicians wholeheartedly embraced him, while the Tories were more disposed to continuing the Stuart line, even if this did mean a Catholic taking the throne.

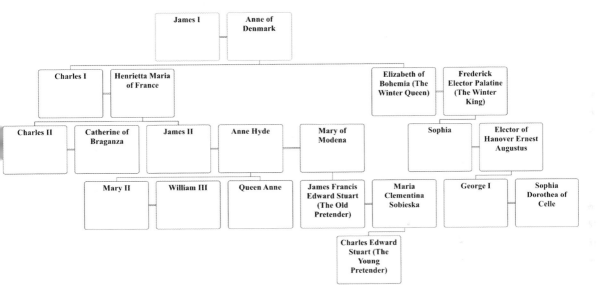

Delayed by bad weather, it was late October before George arrived in London for his coronation and the celebrations for the occasion were accompanied by riots across the land. The Jacobites (supporters of James) mounted a rebellion in 1715, dividing loyalties; the Old Pretender's descendants and adherents would continue to be a thorn in the Hanoverians' side until they were finally crushed by the forces of George II at Culloden more than three decades later.

It didn't help matters that George was unable to speak English, was not fully conversant with English ways and customs and repeatedly over the course of his reign made return visits back to his lands in Hanover, leaving the country in the hands of his council and his eldest son, George Augustus, Prince of Wales… with disastrous results. Father and son were soon at loggerheads and George was fighting dissent on all fronts, in private and in public.

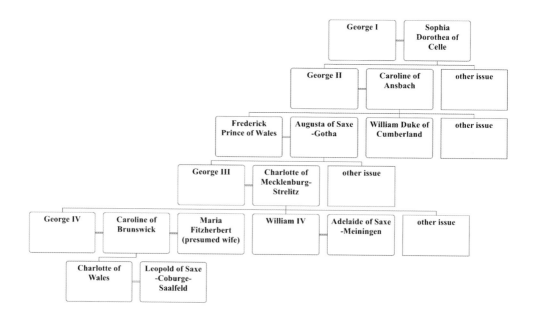

George I died in 1727 while on a tour of his German kingdom; he was buried in Hanover. George Augustus, Prince of Wales, became George II and was received a little more kindly than his father, although his reign too was beset by problems, both in terms of wars and in the heart of his own family. Frederick, Prince of Wales, set himself in opposition to his royal father, repeating the history of the former generation. George II holds the distinction of being the last British monarch to lead an army into battle (at the Battle of Dettingen in 1743 during the War of the Austrian Succession when the British forces supported those of Hanover) and a determined bid by the Old Pretender's son, Charles Edward Stuart (the 'Young Pretender') to gain the crown culminated in the Jacobite rising of 1745.

George II died in 1760 and, his eldest son having predeceased him, his grandson became the new monarch, George III. His was a long reign, again marked by wars (most notably the American and French revolutionary wars) and family fallings-out. Popularly known as 'Farmer George' due to his down-to-earth interest in the common and the everyday (in contrast with his extravagant and spendthrift sons), he is perhaps best remembered for his 'madness' which resulted in George, Prince of Wales, being appointed as regent from 1811 until George III's death in 1820. As for George IV, well, you can read more about him and his excesses in the last chapter of this book.

What a period in history this was! For us it is one of the most fascinating, largely because it so greatly shaped the world we know today. So, make yourself a drink, put your feet up and join us on a trip back in time with this collection of tales from the era.

NB: If you enjoy reading this you might be interested to know that we have also co-authored three historical biographies (you can find further details about them at the end of this book). We also produce a popular, twice-weekly blog, 'All Things Georgian' (hence the title of this book!), and we would love you to join us there. Find us at www.georgianera.wordpress.com

Timeline of Events Relevant to the Long Eighteenth-Century

1714 – George I's reign begins

1715 – The first Doggett's Coat and Badge race on the Thames, also the year of the first Jacobite rising

1727 – Death of George I and the beginning of the reign of George II

1728 – First performance of John Gay's *The Beggar's Opera*

1738 – Birth of the future George III; his father was Frederick, Prince of Wales

1745 – Second Jacobite uprising

1746 – The Battle of Culloden

1751 – Death of Frederick, Prince of Wales, eldest son and heir of George II

1760 – Death of George II; his grandson takes the throne as George III

1761 – The marriage of George III to Princess Charlotte of Mecklenburg-Strelitz

1762 – The birth of George, Prince of Wales, later to become George IV

1764 – Invention of the spinning jenny which industrialized weaving, a key development in the Industrial Revolution

1770 – Captain Cook discovers Botany Bay, Australia

1775 – Start of the American Revolutionary War (War of Independence)

1776 – The signing of the American Declaration of Independence

1781 – Sir William Herschel discovers the planet Uranus

1784 – Marie Élisabeth Thible from Lyons is the first female to ascend in an untethered hot air balloon

1785 – The secret marriage of George, Prince of Wales to Maria Fitzherbert

1789 – The Fall of the Bastille, signalling the start of the French Revolution

1793 – The execution of Louis XVI and Marie Antoinette

1795 – George, Prince of Wales marries Caroline of Brunswick

1796 – The birth of Princess Charlotte, daughter to the Prince and Princess of Wales

1799 – The French Revolution comes to an end

1803 – The Napoleonic Wars begin

1805 – The Battle of Trafalgar

1807 – Slave Trade Act passed in Britain, outlawing the trade of slaves

1811 – The Prince of Wales is appointed Regent due to the madness of his father, George III

1815 – The Battle of Waterloo

1820 – Death of George III and ascension of George IV to the British throne

1821 – Death of Napoléon Bonaparte

1828 – The trial takes place of Burke and Hare, the body-snatchers

1830 – Death of George IV; his younger brother would reign as William IV until 1837

King George I, Sir Godfrey Kneller. (*Yale University Art Gallery*)

Chapter One

Doggett's Coat and Badge

Opinions on the new German king were inherently divided but George I's supporters were vociferous in their support, and one very odd way of celebrating the new reign started a tradition that continues to this very day: the annual Doggett's Coat and Badge race on the Thames which has been held every year since 1715, originally on the anniversary of George's accession to the throne.

Thomas Doggett, a successful Irish comedic actor and theatre manager born c.1650 who had played at Drury Lane and the Haymarket was the instigator of the race. Doggett, a lively little gentleman whose gift for dry humour enlivened many a dinner table, was 'a Whig up to the head and ears' and ardent in his praise for the new king. Honouring George I may have been the sole rationale behind Doggett's plan, although it is also said that one stormy evening the actor was struggling to find a waterman who would take him up river against the tide. At last a young man fresh out of his apprenticeship volunteered his services and this prompted Doggett with the idea of showing both his gratitude to the young waterman and his loyalty to his monarch. The theatres and the watermen relied on each other for their business and it was natural that Doggett should pick this trade to benefit from his wager.

The men who ferried the barges on the Thames were the first public servants to wear a uniform: a pleated coat, knee breeches and a hat, together with a badge or plate on their arm which either denoted their employer or that they had the freedom of the river and were licensed by their guild at Watermen's Hall (all watermen had to serve a seven-year apprenticeship). Informal wagers and races had always been common among the watermen (in 1661 Samuel Pepys recorded one which took the same route as Doggett's) but it was only for the men just out of their apprenticeship that Doggett instigated his Coat and Badge contest; the winner would be granted their freedom by the Watermen's Company and presented with an orange-coloured livery and a silver badge representing 'liberty'. Doggett insisted that the race would be run on the first day of August 'forever' as a commemoration of George I's accession.

The race was open to six watermen who met the qualification and they were to row – against the tide – from the White Swan Tavern by London Bridge to

View of London Bridge, Claude de Jongh. (*Yale Center for British Art, Paul Mellon Fund*)

the Old White Swan at Chelsea, a distance of almost 5 miles. London Bridge, in 1715, still had houses and shops along its length and was a congested thoroughfare from Southwark into the city (it was not until the middle of the century that these buildings were demolished). On the day of the race, spectators began to assemble throughout the afternoon, congregating on the riverside and in the parlour of the Old Swan Tavern which stood next to the Old Swan Stairs (the watermen's stairs which dotted the Thames provided access to and from the barges) and just 'above bridge'. The swift current underneath London Bridge was dangerous and 'shooting the bridge' was rather like going down the rapids; most people crossed the bridge by foot and took a boat again when on the other side.

The race did not begin until the tide against which the men had to row was at its strongest and it could take up to two hours of back-breaking toil before the rowers made the finish line. The winner of the first race was John Opey, a waterman from Bermondsey who plied his trade from St Saviour's Stairs. In 1720, there was contention over a false start to the race and it had to be re-run a few days later; the winner's name has been lost and all is known is that it was a 'below bridge' man from St Catherine's Stairs who won both times. During that race, a spectator fell from the bridge into the river and was drowned. Thomas Doggett was among the huge, pressing crowds and met with his own misfortune:

> As I was making my way through the 'Friars intending to take water at Temple
> Stairs, in order that I might witness the race for my Coat and Badge, one of

View at Chelsea of the Annual Sculling Race for Doggett's Coat and Badge, Edward Francis Burney. (*Yale Center for British Art, Paul Mellon Collection*)

those rake helly fellows that so beset the town, stopped me, and cocking his hat with arms akimbo cried 'Whig or Tory?' He did not care a Queen Anne's farthing for my politics but made it the pretext for a quarrel. I whipped out my hanger [*a short sword*] in a trice, set my back to the wall and cried, 'Hurrah for King George and long life to him', and yet I had liked to have fared scurvily, had I not be thought me that my own name for the nonce would stand me in even better stead than the King's. So when being surrounded by a host of tatterdemalions and pronounced a rat that must bleed, I said be it so my masters and though you fail in the recognition, know that I am Dogget [*sic*], whereat the varlits laughed; true, I escaped with a whole skin, but at the expense of a guinea, this is the gist on't – so now to dinner and afterwards to the White Swan there to drink a cool tankard and shake hands with the winner.

Doggett married Mary Owen, an heiress from Eltham, and retired from the stage. He died – childless – in 1721 and was buried in Eltham churchyard alongside

Jack Broughton, the boxer, John Hamilton Mortimer. (*Yale Center for British Art, Paul Mellon Collection*)

his wife who had predeceased him. Doggett's legacy was his race for which he left provision in his will, determined that it would take place every year; the Fishmongers' Company took over the running of it from 1722 onwards.

Jack Broughton, who later gained fame as the era's foremost pugilist, known as the father of English boxing, initially worked as an apprentice on the Thames and he was the winner in 1730. After gaining his 'freedom' he worked as a waterman from the Hungerford Stairs until able to make his living from his fists instead. Over the years, changes were made to the rules and from 1769 the six men were drawn by lots. Specifications for the barges were standardized as the watermen cunningly began to adapt them for race-day to make their crafts lighter and therefore faster and easier to row. Nowadays, the men and women are chosen by preliminary heats and row with the tide in modern sculling boats. The old London Bridge has been replaced but the race still starts where the Old Swan Stairs were located but, despite Doggett's instructions, the event is no longer held on 1 August, the anniversary of George I's accession to the throne, but instead takes place during the month of July.

Chapter Two

The Venus of Luxembourg

Marie Louise Élisabeth d'Orléans, Duchess of Berry, was born in the summer of 1695 in the Palace of Versailles. Her parents were first cousins; Philippe II, Duke of Orléans, was the son of Louis XIV's younger – and bisexual – brother, Philippe, *Monsieur*, and his second wife, Elizabeth Charlotte of the Palatinate (known as Liselotte) and Louise Élisabeth's mother was Françoise Marie de Bourbon, the youngest illegitimate daughter of Louis XIV and his *maîtresse-en-titre* (chief mistress), Françoise-Athénaïs, Marquise de Montespan. Louise Élisabeth was, therefore, both granddaughter and great-niece to the ageing Sun King.

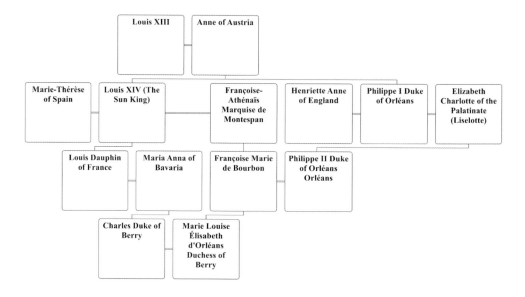

Opposite: Portrait of a Woman, according to tradition Marie Louise Élisabeth d'Orléans, Duchesse de Berry, as Flora, Nicolas de Largillière (school of). (*Rijksmuseum*)

Philippe of Orléans was besotted by his young daughter, nursing Louise Élisabeth through a serious childhood illness and indulging her every whim and wish: his devotion would later lead to slanderous gossip. Her practical and down-to-earth grandmother, Liselotte, the Dowager Duchess of Orléans, disapproved of Louise Élisabeth's lax behaviour but noted that the girl was intelligent, eloquent and had a good heart. She was also tall, handsome and haughty.

In 1710, aged 14, Louise Élisabeth was married to her cousin and the king's grandson, Charles, Duke of Berry who was, for seven years, heir presumptive to the Spanish crown. A year after her marriage, the young Duchess of Berry gave birth to a stillborn daughter. Louise Élisabeth had been advised by her doctors to remain at Versailles but the king would have none of it and insisted she travelled by barge with the court to the Palace of Fontainebleau. It was a traumatic journey: the barge hit a pier and the duchess almost drowned. By this time the marriage between the duke and duchess had also hit the rocks and the duchess had – reputedly – begun to hit the bottle and was gaining a reputation as a glutton:

> The duchesse de Berry fainted dead away. We thought it was a stroke, but when the duchesse de Bourgogne poured some vinegar over her face she returned to her senses and began to vomit abominably. Small wonder, after hours of continuous stuffing during the play – *pêches au caramel*, chestnuts, a confection of redcurrants and cranberries, dried cherries with quantities of lemon – and then she ate some fish for supper and drank on top of that.

On paper, the marriage had been a good match, and the stout but handsome blond-haired duke had been thought a good catch for several of the royal daughters of France, but *Berry bon cœur* ('Berry good heart' as Liselotte termed him) was weak-willed and easily dominated by his headstrong and spoilt young wife. Liselotte was under no illusions as to the state of her granddaughter's union. Three months after their marriage, the duke had fallen in love with a *femme de chambre* (chambermaid), an affair quickly discovered by Louise Élisabeth who blackmailed her husband: if he treated her well, she would turn a blind eye but if he behaved badly she would tell the king and have the maid dismissed. This arrangement suited all very well and held fast almost until the duke's death. Shortly before he expired, the duke had arranged a marriage for his mistress but on the condition that her husband refrained from exercising his conjugal rights. He left both the chambermaid and his duchess pregnant; Louise Élisabeth retained the woman in her service and took care of her and her child.

Opposite: Louis XIV, after Hyacinthe Rigaud. (*The J. Paul Getty Museum (Open Content)*)

Elisabeth Charlotte (Liselotte) of the Palatinate, Duchess of Orléans, workshop of Hyacinthe Rigaud. (© *User: LittleFrog/Wikimedia Commons/CC-BY-SA-3.0*)

The child that the duchess was carrying at her husband's premature death – the result of a fall from his horse – was her third; in 1713 she had produced a sickly son who lived a mere three months. Moreover, in retaliation for the chambermaid who had stolen her husband's affections, Louise Élisabeth had also taken a lover, Monsieur le Haye who had been the king's page but was, at the time of their *amour*, her husband's private *écuyer* or equerry. The duke had been furious, kicking his wife in public and threatening to lock her away in a convent and the duchess had planned to escape to the Netherlands with her lover. She was, therefore, not terribly distraught at being rendered a widow and it is open to debate whether she was carrying her lover's or her husband's child. In the end it mattered not, for the child, another girl, lived for just twelve hours.

The duchess was given the Luxembourg Palace and there the merry young widow presided over increasingly licentious banquets and parties despite being in mourning; to the chagrin of the Parisians, Louise Élisabeth restricted access to the public gardens around the palace. Gambling was rife, and the duchess revelled in presenting *tableaux-vivants* depicting mythological scenes in which she took centre stage as the goddesses Venus and Diana. Nicknamed *Joufflotte* due to her voluptuous and buxom shape, her increasing girth led to rumours that she was pregnant.

Just three weeks after attending a carnival ball at the opera, in February 1716 it was said that the duchess gave birth to a daughter who died days later. Pretending to have a bad cold to explain her confinement, the French papers reported she was in labour, describing Louise Élisabeth as a French Messalina.

The duchess took lovers but the man she was most in thrall to was Armand-Auguste d'Aydie, the Chevalier de Rion, a gentle, polite but penniless officer of dragoons in the king's regiment and in charge of the duchess's company of Guards. Rion was short and chubby with a pimpled, sallow complexion but well-connected: the son of Aimé Blaise d'Aydie, Comte d'Aydie, he boasted the Duke of Lauzun as his great-uncle and the Duke of Biron was his nephew. He was also, according to the gossipy Duke de Saint-Simon, carrying on with one of the duchess's ladies, Madame de Mouchy, the two of them working together to deceive Louise Élisabeth. In the spring of 1717, when she entertained the Russian Tsar, Peter the Great at the Luxembourg Palace, Louise Élisabeth was as 'stout as a tower' and Voltaire was sent to the Bastille for calling her a whore and speculating that she was carrying an incestuous child, the result of an affair with her father who was then the Regent of France.

Louise Élisabeth's debauched life was taking its toll and she prayed at a nearby convent, performing penance to offset her scandalous behaviour.

A year later, the duchess fell pregnant again, with Rion's child, and suffered a difficult labour (it is rumoured that this daughter lived, becoming a nun at the Abbey of Pontoise). Louise Élisabeth was close to death but the priest refused to administer the sacrament while Rion and Madame de Mouchy were in attendance. Secretly, Louise Élisabeth had married the Chevalier de Rion: her enraged father sent him away to fight with the army in Spain when he discovered the union which Liselotte confirmed in a letter, saying Louise Élisabeth's 'marriage with that toad's head is unhappily but too true'. To placate her father, Louise Élisabeth held an open-air supper party for him but caught a chill and lapsed into a fever. She was visited by Liselotte, who found her granddaughter suffering from gout in both feet and in terrible pain.

The doctors' ministrations were to no avail and Louise Élisabeth's health failed alarmingly quickly: she became as thin as she had once been fat and died on 21 July 1719 with her father beside her (it was claimed the autopsy revealed that she was once more *enceinte* (pregnant)). It comes as something of a shock to realize that the young widow was but 23 years of age when she died, having 'made so much noise in the brief space of a very short life'.

A View of the Palace of Versailles towards ye Garden, John Tinney after Jacques Rigaud. (*Yale Center for British Art, Paul Mellon Collection*)

Chapter Three

The Velvet Coffee-Woman

The coffee or chocolate-houses of the eighteenth-century were havens where the clientele, almost exclusively male, could gather to debate, conduct business and keep abreast of the latest news, be it political, financial or everyday gossip.

In 1714, it is said that three coffee-women of Charing Cross were presented to King George I. They were Jenny Man, proprietress (together with Alexander Man) of Old Man's Coffee House (which stood opposite Young Man's Coffee House owned by Hester Man), Mrs Sarah Fenwick (otherwise Moreau), who ran the British Coffee House in Cockspur Street and Mrs Anne Rochford, owner of a coffee or chocolate-house located in, or near to, the King's Mews (the royal stables located at the southern end of St Martin's Lane). The ladies appeared – somewhat scandalously – dressed in velvet as though they were nobility and not working-women (landlady of a coffee-house was a profession often equated with prostitution, the only women in the building usually being the proprietress and her serving girls). It was a cruel prank to play upon the new king who spoke little

Figures in a Tavern or Coffee House, attributed to Joseph Highmore. (*Yale Center for British Art, Paul Mellon Collection*)

English and was still learning the customs of his new kingdom and so the king was well and truly duped when the women were brought before him (by a disreputable duke who has remained nameless).

All three coffee-women addressed the king in turn. Jenny, whose house was popular with officers, especially those on half-pay, pleaded her interest with the army, while Mrs Fenwick spoke of her influence over the Scottish highland clans as her emporium was frequented by the many Scots in London. Anne Rochford, however, spoke to the king of love:

> Excuse me, cry'd *Nan*,
> (For at length she began)
> If I plead not so well; by this Light;
> But let mine be the Prize,
> And a Word to the Wise,
> You're welcome at *Rochford's* each night.
>
> And there I'll present You,
> The more to content You,
> (At least, if a Female can do't)
> With a Bottle, and Whore,
> With Oysters good store,
> And pay your two Chairmen to Boot.

Nan Rochford won the day. She was in favour of the new Hanoverian king: an old tale recalls that when a gentleman asked her why the Whigs in their mourning for Queen Anne all wore silk stockings, she replied with a clever pun: 'because the Tories were worsted.'

Jacobite riots had broken out in London during April 1715, and later that year John Erskine, Earl of Mar raised the Old Pretender's standard at Braemar in Aberdeenshire. Against this backdrop, Joseph Addison, playwright, poet and politician, launched *The Freeholder*, a short-lived bi-weekly political news sheet addressed to the men who were freeholders (i.e. entitled to vote) and in support of the Whig administration. Several of the articles in *The Freeholder* were addressed to the womenfolk of those male voters and, in one of the later issues, Addison inferred that women who opposed the Hanoverian regime (and supported the Tories) were prostitutes. Anne Rochford – or someone using her identity – continued the argument in a pamphlet titled *Nanny Roc[hfor]d's Letter to a member of the B[ee]f Stake Club, in vindication of certain ladies calumniated in the Freeholder of March 9th*. Anne – equated with the profession of whore or bawd – was scathing, 'for I declare, I had rather be show'd Naked, like *Lazarillo*, even for a *Sea-Monster*, than be marked out for a *Tory*.'

Charing Cross, with the Statue of King Charles I and Northumberland House, Joseph Nickolls. (*Yale Center for British Art, Paul Mellon Collection*)

As a reward for her love and loyalty, the royal favour ensured a high-class clientele at Mrs Rochford's establishment in the Royal Mews, which branched out, selling not just coffee, tea and chocolate but punch and spirits as well.

Anne was born in the early 1680s, at Deal in Kent. Her father, Francis Voss, tall, handsome and well-educated (for his station in life), had been at sea with Arthur Herbert, 1st Earl of Torrington. Landing in Deal from a sea voyage with the earl, Francis met a pretty young woman who lived in a farmhouse near the coastal town and paid her several visits, promising marriage in return for certain favours. Alas, Francis played false. After Anne's birth nine months later, Francis abandoned her mother and settled at Lambeth where he found employment as a waterman and retained the position as Master of Lord Torrington's barge. In time, he married again and when news of this reached Deal, his former mistress died of grief. Sadly for young Anne, her father soon followed her mother to the grave and left everything he owned to his wife, Sarah, who remained a widow for five years before remarrying to George Weston, another Lambeth waterman.

Anne found employment as a nursery maid to a City of London merchant and often took her charges to the Old Swan Stairs to ask the watermen for news of her stepmother. Then, in October 1707 and at St Clement Danes in Westminster, Anne married James Rochford, a widower whose name she would bear for the rest of her life. While the union was short-lived, Anne prospered financially and, by 1713, was mistress of her coffee-house, notorious enough to be one of the three coffee-women presented to the king the following year.

A certain colonel was enamoured of Mrs Anne Rochford, now passing (whether in truth or not) as a widow, and showered her with money and presents. Anne's star was at its zenith; when her stepmother suffered financial difficulties, Anne was able to help. Sarah Weston had inherited two houses in Stangate, Lambeth (between Lambeth Palace and Westminster Bridge although, in the 1710s, the bridge was yet to be constructed). It was an area of the Thames shoreline dotted with barge houses belonging to the nobility, including the King's Barge House. Anne took over the leases, repairing the decaying properties and building two more houses adjoining. With the profits, she allowed her stepmother enough money to live comfortably.

Thames at Lambeth Palace, unknown artist. (*Yale Center for British Art, Paul Mellon Collection*)

Just as quickly as it had risen, Anne's star now fell to earth. She met a roguish Irishman named MacDermot one day while strolling through Hyde Park, an imposter who claimed to be of ancient lineage and descended from the kings of Munster. He quickly replaced the colonel in Anne's affections but, sadly for our heroine, MacDermot was a wastrel. In no time he helped Anne to run through her money so quickly that she had to mortgage her houses: she gave him his marching orders, told him that she could no longer support his extravagancies and the couple parted, but Anne's life had now reached its conclusion. Perhaps hastened to her grave by her woes, Anne died in August 1727 aged 45 of a 'mortification in her bowels' and lays buried in the middle aisle of Lambeth church. (George I had died in June of the same year, to be succeeded on the throne by his eldest son, George II.)

NB: Anne's maiden surname is given in a 1728 pamphlet of her life as Woase, otherwise Voyce, but was actually Voss or Vosse.

Chapter Four

Crazy Sally: A Female Bonesetter

Bonesetters, as the name suggests, set dislocated and broken bones. Usually unqualified, bonesetters were also almost exclusively men.

Sarah Wallen – known as Sally – was born c.1706 in the Wiltshire village of Hindon, the second of four children. Her father was a bonesetter and Sally

Sarah Mapp née Wallen, George Cruikshank, after William Hogarth. (*Wellcome Collection*)

followed in his footsteps. Heavy-set – if the caricature of her that exists is accurate – and with phenomenal brute strength for a woman, Sally was the antithesis of her younger sister Maria who we will soon meet within these pages: Maria Wallen changed her surname to Warren and found fame on the stage, principally in the role of Polly Peachum in *The Beggar's Opera*. Sally's life took a very different course.

Leaving her Wiltshire home and travelling across the country, Sally ended up in the pretty market town of Epsom in Surrey where she first found fame as a bonesetter and became known as 'Cracked – or Crazy – Sally, the One and Only Bonesetter'. Perhaps her nickname had something to do with her altruism, for Sally refused to accept more than a crown for curing her poorer patients, even though her growing fame meant that she could charge much more (sometimes she waived her fee altogether); for her wealthy patients, she charged a guinea.

Epsom was an ideal place for Sally to ply her trade; it was well-known for horse-racing and so there was a plentiful supply of broken bones from tumbles on the turf and a constant stream of high society there to watch the races. Her notoriety

The Duke of Rutland's Bonny Black, John Wootton. (*Yale Center for British Art, Paul Mellon Collection*)

The Grecian Coffee House, Devereux Court, the Strand, George Shepheard. (*Yale Center for British Art, Paul Mellon Collection*)

spread to the capital and soon her services were in high demand, so much that, rather than lose her to London, the people of Epsom formed a subscription to offer her up to 300 guineas a year to remain in their town. Within a short time, crowds were flocking to Epsom not just to witness the action on the turf, but to see Crazy Sally. It was reported that she was earning 20 guineas a day and, despite her lack of ambition, she became rich as well as famous. Sally acquired a carriage and travelled to London one day every week to treat patients at the Grecian Coffee House in Devereux Court. The noted physician Hans Sloane (who counted George I and II among his patients) came to watch her work and she treated his niece's crooked back. Many people thought that Sally was a quack, nothing more than a charlatan who managed to fool people by sometimes managing – by luck more than by good judgement – to reset bones due to her brute strength alone. To trick Sally, a man pretending to have a broken wrist was sent to be tended by her but the skilful Sally had the measure of him. After examining the man's wrist, she swiftly dislocated it and ordered him to go back to the fools who had sent him and get them to reset the bone.

Sally's fame now gained her a husband. On 4 August 1736, at All Hallows church in the City of London, she married a man named Hill Mapp.

Hill Mapp was a footman to Ebenezer Ibbetson, a mercer of Ludgate Hill in London. Sally had worked her magic upon Mr Ibbetson's daughter (who had been lame for some years) and while in the house she took a liking to Mr Mapp. Despite the opposition of her friends, she decided that he was to be her husband. The date was set and Sally took lodgings in London before her wedding; almost twenty gentlemen's carriages were seen outside, such was her fame. After the marriage, Sally and her new husband returned to Epsom where she continued to act as a bonesetter.

The marriage – as Sally's friends had predicted – was a disaster. The newspapers reported that he had another wife living with whom he had two children and soon Hill Mapp vanished, taking Sally's savings with him. Sally was pragmatic and thought it good riddance. Now at the zenith of her fame, she was invited to Kensington Palace and presented to George II's wife Queen Caroline and, while in London, was mistaken for the Duchess of Kendal and Munster, Ehrengard Melusine von der Schulenburg who had been George I's German mistress. Even though George I was long since dead, the duchess was still disliked by the public and a mob began to bay at Mrs Mapp who was finely dressed in a *robe de chambre* and travelling in her new coach. Enraged, Sally stuck her head out of her coach and accosted them: 'Damn your bloods, don't you know me? I am Mrs Mapp the bonesetter', upon which the jeers turned to huzzahs.

Sadly, Sally Mapp's fame dissipated just as quickly as it had manifested itself. It is reputed that she began to drink. Unless there were two men going by the

name of Hill Mapp in London at the time, in July 1737 her feckless and possibly bigamous husband married – as a bachelor – Miss Hester Rushton at St Gregory by St Paul's in the City of London. Given the closeness to his previous address, Mr Mapp perhaps viewed his union with Sally as non-binding and so maybe it had never been consummated. Sally was now a figure of fun, a situation made worse when she was caricatured by none other than Hogarth himself, depicted as ugly and brutish, dressed in a harlequin's costume. She died during December 1737, in poverty, at her lodgings at Seven Dials in London, afforded just a pauper's burial.

Opposite: Caroline Wilhelmina of Brandenburg-Ansbach, Consort to George II, unknown artist. (*Retford Town Hall, Bassetlaw District Council*)

Chapter Five

The Polly Peerage

On 29 January 1728, John Gay's *The Beggar's Opera* opened at the Lincoln's Inn Fields Theatre in London. It was an instant success and made stars of its performers, in particular a young actress named Lavinia Fenton who had been plucked from the London streets and placed on the stage. *The Beggar's Opera* turned her into an overnight sensation.

The Beggar's Opera, William Hogarth. (*Yale Center for British Art, Paul Mellon Collection*)

Lavinia Fenton, later Duchess of Bolton, as Polly Peachum in John Gay's *The Beggar's Opera*,
Charles Jervas. (© *Jan Arkesteijn/Wikimedia Commons/CC-BY-SA-3.0*)

The opera was described as a *Newgate pastoral*, a satire depicting thieves and whores and poking fun at notorious criminals, politicians and personalities including – in a curious twist, as we shall discover – the Whig statesman, Sir Robert Walpole, 1st Earl of Orford.

Lavinia took on the role of Polly Peachum, the daughter of Mr Peachum, a tavern landlord and leader of a gang of criminals. Polly falls in love with the anti-hero of the opera, Macheath, a highwayman. Her innocent and youthful beauty garnered Lavinia a veritable army of male admirers, chief among them Charles Powlett, 3rd Duke of Bolton who attended the theatre nightly, so often, in fact, that when William Hogarth painted a scene from *The Beggar's Opera*, depicting Lavinia as Polly on the stage, the duke was shown in a box to the right. Well and truly captivated, the duke cared nothing for Lavinia's lowly birth: reputedly illegitimate, her father was said to be a naval lieutenant named Beswick who sailed before she was born, leaving behind nothing but an empty promise to return and wed her mother. When he failed to do so, 'Mrs Beswick' married a Mr Fenton instead, a coffee-house keeper from Charing Cross. The truth is a little more prosaic: during May 1710, Peter Beswick, a widowed victualler, married Elizabeth Neal at Wapping in the East End of London. Their daughter, Lavinia, was born almost exactly five months later and christened at St Margaret's in Westminster. Legend says that, as a young adolescent, Lavinia tried out the roles of whore, waitress and barmaid in turn before taking to the stage but once in the spotlight, she proved to be a natural actress, clever and witty with a vivacious personality.

The smitten duke took Lavinia off the stage and into his keeping, and they lived happily together, Lavinia bearing her noble beau three sons. When the duke's estranged wife finally died, he married Lavinia with haste and so she was raised to the peerage as the Duchess of Bolton.

Lavinia was replaced on the stage by Maria Warren (really Wallen, Crazy Sally's sister and a bonesetter's daughter from Hindon in Wiltshire).

Miss Warren was deemed a very pretty replacement for the celebrated Miss Fenton and soon she too had her pick from an array of male suitors. Perhaps a little more 'respectable' than her forebear, Maria chose to marry rather than be any man's mistress but went about it in a haphazard manner that saw her end up in the dock of the Old Bailey. Eight months after first appearing as Polly, on St Valentine's Day, Maria made a clandestine marriage at the King's Arms Tavern on Ludgate Hill to John Sommers, a Gloucestershire gentleman. Two months later she married once again, this time in a church – St. Benet's, Paul's Wharf in the City of London – but to a different man, a wealthy gentleman named George Nicholas. Neither man was by her side when, in December 1736, Maria – long past her theatrical heyday – was charged with bigamy. Luckily for her, she was acquitted on a technicality as the only proof of her first clandestine marriage having taken place was the Fleet

Captain Macheath Upbraided by Polly and Lucy in *The Beggar's Opera*, Gilbert Stuart Newton. (*Yale Center for British Art, Paul Mellon Collection*)

Register, in which the location had been entered incorrectly and then overwritten so the ceremony could not be established beyond reasonable doubt.

Following Maria's two marriages and removal from the stage, the role of Polly Peachum was soon filled by Hannah Norsa, noted as the first Jewish actress to tread the boards in London. Her father owned a succession of chocolate-houses and taverns in Covent Garden and so Hannah grew up surrounded by the theatres and acting folk, entranced by their fame and glamour. She was probably no more than 18 years of age when she took to the stage, and the pretty new Polly Peachum attracted the beaux just as much as her forebears had done in the role. She soon had her own titled lover. Robert, Viscount Walpole was the eldest son and heir of the Earl of Orford, the Whig statesman who was lampooned in *The Beggar's Opera*. Like the Duke of Bolton, Viscount Walpole was trapped in an unhappy marriage and it was not long before history repeated itself. Hannah relinquished the role of Polly to live as her titled lover's mistress, reigning supreme at the magnificent Houghton Hall in Norfolk, Walpole's stately home after he had ascended to the earldom on his father's death. One son, named Robert, was born to the couple (in 1740) but he died young and unfortunately for Hannah, Walpole's estranged wife outlived him and so Miss Norsa never gained a countess's coronet. Far from benefiting from her tenure as the 2nd Earl of Orford's mistress, Hannah was reportedly left in

Covent Garden, Pieter Angillis. (*Yale Center for British Art, Paul Mellon Collection*)

debt after he died; it was rumoured that Walpole had squandered a £3,000 legacy Hannah had received from her father, whose business empire had gone from strength to strength. Seeing out her days in the Netherlands before returning to London, Hannah proved she had, in fact, inherited her father's financial acumen after all. Her last will and testament revealed that she died a very wealthy woman and possibly her claims of penury had been her finest acting performance, designed to keep her inheritance from her father safe from her lover's creditors who had been pressing for repayment of his considerable debts.

Chapter Six

Cecil Court on Fire

Cecil Court was – and still is – a narrow thoroughfare dating from the late seventeenth-century linking the bustling St Martin's Lane and Castle Street (now Charing Cross Road) in the heart of Covent Garden. A passageway led from Cecil Court into St Martin's Court behind and Old Slaughter's Coffee House was just around the corner. The great eighteenth-century painter William Hogarth knew the narrow Cecil Court well: it connected his town house in Leicester Fields (now Leicester Square) with the academy he established in 1735 on St Martin's Lane. Among the terraced houses in Cecil Court was a cook's shop run by a woman named Eleanor Pickhaver and, next door, Elizabeth Calloway

William Hogarth, self-portrait. (*Yale Center for British Art, Paul Mellon Collection*)

Great Fire of London, Philippe-Jacques de Loutherbourg. (*Yale Center for British Art, Paul Mellon Collection*)

ran a brandy shop and lodging house. In the same year that Hogarth began his St Martin's Academy, Elizabeth Calloway's house was destroyed in a dreadful fire that began half an hour before midnight on the evening of 9 June and spread quickly.

The Great Fire of London, which started in a bakery on Pudding Lane in 1666, was still within living memory. Panic set in when it was realized Elizabeth's house was on fire. She was not at home, her brandy shop was closed for the evening and the only occupants were three people who lodged in the cellar of the house: Elizabeth Charley, her daughter and young grandson. Elizabeth Calloway had invited the Charley family to join her that evening away from Cecil Court, but the old lady was tired and refused the invitation. Instead, all three were asleep when the fire took hold and did not instantly realize what was happening, putting the commotion from the upper floors down to the usual hubbub from the brandy shop. Their cellar soon filled with smoke but they escaped with their lives.

Outside was a scene of chaos. The ground and second floors of Elizabeth's house were well ablaze but – oddly – the first floor was still free of flames. People were stirring from their beds and rushing to help quell the inferno and retrieve as many possessions as humanly possible from the adjoining houses before they too caught fire. Several brandy casks were brought out of Elizabeth Calloway's house which were discovered to be empty, a fact that would later cast suspicion on the landlady. Frederick, Prince of Wales (George II's eldest son who was estranged from his royal parents) turned up with a detachment of Foot Guards to direct the fire engines and assist the rescue effort. Under cover of the panic, looters ran back and forth into the houses, making off with anything that looked valuable. It was pandemonium. Elizabeth's house was lost, as were the neighbouring houses belonging to Simon Batty and Richard Monk and others in St Martin's Court behind. Several families lost their entire worldly possessions and were left destitute. There was one fatality, attributed indirectly to the fire. Mrs Anne Hogarth, the artist's widowed mother, died of fright.

Elizabeth Calloway was supping good Sussex beer in the Lodge at the King's Mews when she heard the commotion and saw the sky glowing, indicating a fire. Going to the gate, Elizabeth paled and exclaimed 'Lord! How light it is here in the Mews. I wish it may not be in our Court.' She had only been there for fifteen minutes; the fire had started almost as soon as she had left her house. A boy was sent to find out more but failed to return and Elizabeth left around midnight, seemingly untroubled.

A young, unmarried woman striving to survive in the harsh London streets, Elizabeth Calloway was 24 years old. She had been partially educated at the Grey Coat School in St Margaret's, Westminster where the poor of the parish could receive a meagre education and although she left unable to read or write, Elizabeth was taught the skills that would prepare her for a life of domestic service. At the age of 14, she was apprenticed for five years to a man named Cotton, a waterman who lived in Dirty Lane, really Lindsey Lane, close by her school.

After serving her apprenticeship in Dirty Lane, Elizabeth moved in with a Mrs Greet who lived in nearby Masham Street. There Elizabeth remained for three years, unwaged but somehow, by fair means or foul, managing to pay for her board and lodgings, feed and clothe herself. We will leave it to the reader's imagination to wonder just how Elizabeth earned her crust.

By 1735, Elizabeth's name appeared on the rate books for a property in Cecil Court. Although she had moved out of Mrs Greet's house, Claudius Meldicott, one of her lodgers, claimed that Elizabeth did not sleep at her new address for more than four nights every month. Usually Elizabeth's front door was closed between

Frederick, Prince of Wales, Charles Philips. (*Yale Center for British Art, Paul Mellon Collection*)

9 and 10 o'clock in the evening, leaving her clientele inside, drinking, smoking, swearing and running up and down stairs till the early hours of the morning according to the next-door neighbour, Mary Batty, although one of Elizabeth's lodgers swore that he never saw any disorder in the house: Elizabeth kept regular hours and never served anyone who was already drunk. Always very careful about the risk of fire, Elizabeth constantly warned her lodgers to take care with their candles and, as it was summer, had not had a fire in her house for some time. She was worried though about Eleanor Pickhaver's cook's shop next door. The wainscot in a closet in Elizabeth's room, on the adjoining wall between her house and the cook's shop, regularly got frighteningly hot and so, against the risk of a fire, Elizabeth insured her property for £150. It was a high amount and Elizabeth freely admitted to a friend that she often 'had not the value of twenty shillings in her shop, tho' sometimes she had more'.

Suspicion immediately fell on Elizabeth. The fire had taken hold no more than five minutes after Elizabeth had closed her front door and disappeared down Castle Street to the Mews, she had made sure that she and most of her lodgers were out and that her brandy shop was closed, the casks rescued on the night were as empty as the shop and due to the insurance policy, Elizabeth stood to recoup her losses, in stark contrast to her neighbours. Eleanor Pickhaver was quick to point the finger of blame at her young neighbour, with whom she was at loggerheads. Five or six weeks earlier, Elizabeth had accused Mrs Pickhaver of selling meat that was full of sand to a woman she had sent round for six pence worth of boiled beef:

> I bid the woman leave what she brought if she did not like it. She went back, and [Elizabeth Calloway] came in a hurry, and said, 'Hussy, keep my money at your peril, I'll soon cure ye of selling meat here'.

With all the evidence pointing towards arson, Elizabeth was arrested and hauled to Newgate to await trial at the Old Bailey. In much the same way that suspicion had fallen upon foreigners and Catholics living in London in the wake of the Great Fire of 1666, the newspapers branded Elizabeth an Irishwoman and a papist who had threatened to 'have a bonfire that should warm all her rascally neighbours'. Her fate appeared to be sealed.

Elizabeth was charged in the Old Bailey with 'maliciously setting on fire her own dwelling-house, with an intent to burn the houses of Simon Batty and Richard Monk, and thereby did set on fire and burn the houses of the said Batty and Monk.' First up in the witness box was Elizabeth's lodger of two years, Claudius Meldicott; he was the man with whom she had visited and drunk beer on the night of the fire (possibly he worked as a porter at the King's Mews). Meldicott had invited Elizabeth down to his lodge the night before, but she had forgotten about the invitation. He asked her again the next day and as another of her lodgers,

The Mews, after Thomas Malton. (*Yale Center for British Art, Paul Mellon Collection*)

Thomas Lucas, had just paid his rent, Elizabeth, a generous landlady when she had the means, agreed to meet Meldicott with her other lodgers in order to treat them all to a drink. With the brandy shop temporarily closed for the evening, the merry party at the King's Mews Lodge consisted of Elizabeth, her lodgers, Claudius Meldicott and Thomas Lucas (a 'lusty foot soldier'), together with their respective wives, and Luke and Susan Clark who were neighbours in Cecil Court (Susan had previously lodged for a year with Elizabeth). They had left Cecil Street in ones and twos with Elizabeth being the last to lock up and leave as she was worried someone might realize that the house was empty and break in.

A customer at the brandy shop, Elizabeth Atkins, testified that she had supplied material that could have been used for kindling:

Elizabeth Atkins:	I went for a dram at the Prisoner's House about a fortnight before the fire, and she desired me to fetch her four brushes, which I did, and she said they were to air her room.
Elizabeth Calloway:	She did fetch me four faggots, sure enough.
Elizabeth Atkins:	They were not faggots, they were brushes, such as they have to kindle fires with.

With the prosecution finished, things did not look good for Elizabeth. The inference was that she had deliberately set fire to her house in order to fraudulently claim on her insurance policy, exaggerating her claim by pretending that the empty brandy casks had been full. In committing her crime, she had recklessly endangered the lives of her lodgers in the cellar and her neighbour's houses, and indirectly caused the death of the elderly Mrs Hogarth.

The judge and jury now listened to Elizabeth's defence. It was proved that she had been invited to join Meldicott, thereby allaying the suspicion that her presence at his lodge was part of her grand plan, and also that she was in the habit of treating her lodgers to a beer or two when she was flush with cash. There was nothing unusual in her behaviour on the night. The friends with whom she had been drinking all spoke in favour of their landlady and friend. Although they agreed that she had probably overestimated the value of her possessions on her insurance policy, Margaret Lucas gave a reasonable explanation for the empty brandy casks. The ones on the upper shelves of the brandy shop were there only for show. A friend, Mary Bushel, had stayed with Elizabeth in her room at the Cecil Court house and recalled that the closet got alarmingly hot from the cook's shop next door and Luke Clark confirmed that Elizabeth had told him some months earlier that this was the reason she had taken out the insurance. Six other witnesses all said they did not believe Elizabeth would set fire to a house.

The jury found Elizabeth Calloway not guilty.

They also found Mary Steward alias Young not guilty. Mary lived in a cellar in Cecil Court and, in the confusion and because of the 'hurry and fright she was in' took a bed and three pictures belonging to Richard Monk in place of her own. William Gordon was burned out of his house and then successfully duped by two young women. Eleanor Plasty, his former servant, came to 'help' on the night and left with six curtains and five china dishes. Gordon then took rooms in Cranbourn Alley and, at Plasty's instigation, hired a friend of hers as his servant: Mary Lloyd, who had forged her reference. She soon absconded with what few belongings the Gordons had left. The jury was disposed to mercy and acquitted the pair of them. James Newby was not so lucky. He stole an iron pin and three iron bars during the fire and was sentenced to transportation.

As for Elizabeth, she found herself lodging back in St Margaret's, Westminster in the house of a Mrs Lloyd in Duke Street, York Buildings. There Elizabeth, once again with no discernible wage coming in but possibly living on the money left from her insurance claim, stayed for 'near a twelvemonth' before she was admitted, on 19 February 1738, to the workhouse in St Martin's, just a short distance from her former home in Cecil Court. When she recounted her history to the board of governors, Elizabeth wisely and carefully neglected to give any information regarding her life or whereabouts during 1735 and 1736 lest assistance be withheld.

Chapter Seven

Jenny Cameron:
The Jacobite Mystery of a Female Imposter

During July 1749, the town of Newcastle was excited by the arrival of a woman – a 'Female Imposter' – who was brought from Durham jail wearing men's clothing and committed to the House of Correction. She gave differing versions of her back story: to some, she claimed to be a 'squire's daughter of considerable fortune' from the area around Alnwick in Northumberland; to others she said she was the daughter of a gentleman who lived near Carlisle.

Her education had taken place in Newcastle, at 'the best Needle and Pastry Schools'. (Pastry Schools were common in Scotland but not so much over the border; they had been tried without success in London during the middle of the eighteenth-century.)

> In the best families in town, the education of daughters was fitted, not only to embellish and improve their minds; but to accomplish them in the useful and necessary arts of domestic economy. The sewing school, the pastry school, were then essential branches of female education.

Afterwards, this 'female imposter' was sent to a boarding school in York from where she was married to a Captain Drummond of the (Jacobite) Duke of Perth's Regiment. The Duke of Perth, himself a Drummond, had been brought up and educated in France; his grandfather, James Drummond, the 4th Earl of Perth, had taken part in the Jacobite Rising of 1715 and had been stripped of his peerage as a result. The title of Duke of Perth was conferred on him by the Old Pretender, James Edward Stuart, but the British government and crown did not officially recognize the title.

In 1745, the Young Pretender, Charles Edward Stuart – otherwise Bonnie Prince Charlie – sailed from France to the Western Isles and made his way to the Scottish mainland (his father had decided he was too old for the fight). At Glenfinnan, surrounded by a gathering army from the clans of MacDonalds, Camerons, Macfies and MacDonnells and in defiance of King George II, the prince raised his standard and claimed the Scottish, Irish and English thrones in the name of his father.

Opposite: George II, unknown artist. (*Retford Town Hall, Bassetlaw District Council*)

The Jacobite army marched south into England during the latter months of 1745, reaching Derby before turning back and retreating to Scotland, where the decisive Battle of Culloden was fought on 16 April 1746 and the Bonnie Prince's rebel army was defeated. The prince fled to an island in the Outer Hebrides, from where, disguised as an Irish spinning maid named Betty Burke and with the assistance of a plucky local girl, Flora MacDonald, he escaped from under the noses of the Hanoverian army to Skye. While the Young Pretender eventually boarded a French frigate and sailed for the safety of France, Flora was arrested and – for a time – held in the Tower of London.

By the time of Culloden, our heroine claimed that she had borne two children to Captain Drummond while living with him in France. She left the youngsters there when she returned with her husband, donning male attire and fighting alongside him at Culloden: she survived but with injuries to her face; her husband lost his life. Since then she had travelled from town to town, telling her story and garnering sympathy and charity in equal measure, drawing 'tears of compassion from some of [her] sex, to see a person of her rank in a correction house, lying on straw'. She sometimes suggested that her name was Miss Jenny Cameron and said that she was 'resolved to wear Men's Cloaths all her Life'.

The Battle of Culloden, near Inverness in Scotland, unknown artist. (*Yale Center for British Art, Paul Mellon Collection*)

Alongside Flora MacDonald, Jenny (or Jeannie) Cameron has entered into Jacobite myth and legend, a composite of two women who shared the name. The first Jenny was the daughter of Cameron of Glendessary and the wife of an Irishman named O'Neill, although she had left him and returned to the Highlands and her maiden name. A 'genteel, well-looking, handsome woman, with a pair of pretty eyes and hair as black as jet' and in her mid- to late-40s, Jenny came to Glenfinnan to represent her brothers and to watch the raising of the standard, and gifted

Jenny Cameron. (*National Library of Scotland, Jacobite Prints and Broadsides*)

several Highland cows to the Young Pretender, although she never personally met him. Her presence was widely reported, and her name gained a certain notoriety. Afterwards, she returned home, looked after her brother's estate and died in 1772 at Mount Cameron, Lanarkshire.

While Bonnie Prince Charlie was at Stirling Castle in early 1746, a second Miss (or Mrs) Jenny Cameron took her place in the drama. This second Jenny was an Edinburgh milliner who travelled to Stirling to visit a relative injured while serving in the Highland army. With the English forces approaching, commanded by Prince William, Duke of Cumberland (nicknamed The Butcher, he was George II's youngest son), the Jacobites decamped north but Jenny's relative couldn't be moved and she stayed by his side, still there when Cumberland's forces arrived and took her prisoner. The duke, when hearing her name, confused her with the former Miss Cameron. He wrote from Stirling on 2 February 1746: 'We have taken about twenty of their sick here, and the famous Miss Jenny Cameron, whom I propose to send to Edinburgh for the Lord Justice Clerk to examine.'

Jenny Cameron was duly sent to Edinburgh Castle where she remained for most of the year until being released. During her incarceration, a scurrilous pamphlet was circulated, purporting to be a biography, *A Brief Account of the Life and Family of*

West View of the City of Edinburgh, unknown artist after Paul Sandby. (*Yale Center for British Art, Paul Mellon Collection*)

Miss Jenny Cameron, the Reputed Mistress of the Pretender's Eldest Son, containing many very singular incidents, and identifying her as the former Jenny, sister and daughter of Mr Cameron of Glendessary. Many of these 'singular incidents' involved the heroine disguising herself in men's clothing and, like the 'female imposter' in Newcastle, the Jenny in the pamphlet lived for a while in France, where she had a child. Although it suggested many dark deeds had taken place, the pamphlet ended by discrediting popular rumours that Jenny had been the Young Pretender's mistress, claiming that her age – she was almost 50 – secured her from the scandal.

However, the rumours persisted and when the second Jenny reopened her Edinburgh milliner's shop, business boomed in the mistaken belief that she had enjoyed the prince's affections.

The poor woman in Newcastle wasn't so lucky. It was discovered, after enquiries, that she had been 'no more than a basket wench, who used to carry meat from the butchers to gentlemen's families, to carry coals, clean houses, or hawk fruit through the streets [of Newcastle], and associate with the worst of company'.

She was remembered as first appearing in the town during 1744 or 1745, dressed in a sailor's jacket and breeches, claiming to have been a sailor for many years and owning herself a Catholic, so it was thought probable that she had been involved in the rebellion. Her name was Sarah Waugh and the scars she bore explained as the result of 'a rowelling when young, to extract some frantick humours from her brain, which began to appear very early' and as the result of a fall. She had possibly been held in Bedlam (Bethlem Hospital) in London. After being examined by the Newcastle magistrates, Sarah was issued with a vagrant's pass to 'Kirby-Gate, in the Parish of Alson [Alston] in Cumberland, the place of her settlement'.

Was there any truth at all in the story given by the female imposter in men's clothing who had arrived in Newcastle via Durham jail? We'll leave you with a story preserved in folklore about one of the two Jenny Camerons. A gentleman was buying snuff in an Edinburgh shop when a beggar entered. The shopkeeper gave the beggar a groat and the poor man took it and left, never uttering a single word either in supplication or thanks. The gentleman had, however, noticed that the arm the beggar extended to receive the coin was slender and delicate and he quizzed the shopkeeper who admitted that the beggar, although dressed in men's clothing, was no man but in fact 'Jeanie Cameron', who had followed the Young Pretender to France only to lose the prince's favour as well as that of her family when she returned, dejectedly, to Scotland. A different source recalls:

> Jeanie Cameron, the mistress of Prince Charles Edward, was seen by an old acquaintance of ours standing upon the streets of Edinburgh, about the year '86. She was dressed in men's clothes and had a wooden leg. This celebrated and once attractive beauty, whose charms and Amazonian gallantry had captivated a prince, afterwards died in a stair-foot somewhere in the Canongate.

Was this, then, the fate of Jenny Cameron the Edinburgh milliner?

Chapter Eight

The Queen's Ass

What do you give someone who has everything for a wedding present? Well, a zebra, of course.

In 1762 a pair of Cape Mountain zebras, the smallest of their kind, were sent aboard HMS *Terpsichore*, captained by Sir Thomas Adams. The two animals were a belated wedding gift from the governor of the Cape of Good Hope to Queen Charlotte who had married King George III on 8 September 1761. Sadly, the male died during the journey, but the female, with a beautiful variegated skin, arrived safe and sound.

> From her mane to her tail is a streak of black, from which descend on each side alternate rays of black and white, about two inches broad. She is an animal of the horse kind, with a small head and very long ears.

The zebra was kept in the menagerie at Buckingham House (also known as the Queen's House and later Buckingham Palace) before being moved to Kensington in September 1762. Naturally, such an unusual animal sparked the interest of the masses and became an overnight celebrity, so much so that people arrived day and night to see it at three pence a visit and a sentinel and guard had to be placed at the door of her stable.

The creature, somewhat disrespectfully, became known as 'the Queen's Ass'. You can almost hear people saying that they were 'off to see the Queen's Ass'.

The downside of visiting 'the Queen's Ass' was that it proved a popular haunt for pickpockets; there were numerous reports of people having their money and other items stolen while admiring the zebra but, but even more worrying, the sentinels who were guarding the zebra were extorting money from people eager to gain closer access to the new and interesting creature. The guards were ultimately given very strict warnings that such unbecoming behaviour would not be tolerated.

Eventually, in 1765 the female zebra and an elephant were moved to the Royal Menagerie in the Tower of London. Admission to the spectacle cost just a few pennies or – somewhat gruesomely – the provision of a cat or dog to be fed to the

Opposite: Queen Charlotte, Allan Ramsay. (*The Indianapolis Museum of Art at Newfields*)

Zebra (The Queen's Ass), George Stubbs. (*Yale Center for British Art, Paul Mellon Collection*)

Buckingham House in St James's Park from the side of the canal near Rosamond's Pond, unknown artist. (*Yale Center for British Art, Paul Mellon Collection*)

ZEBRA

The QUEENS.———

Publ April 17.1787 by SW Fores at the Caracature Warehouse Nº3 Piccadilly

lions that were also held in the menagerie. The presence of the zebra would have served to fill the royal coffers, although it became a subject for mockery later with caricatures using the zebra as a symbol of both stupidity and gluttony! The Prince Regent, later George IV, was more than once depicted in a striped suit looking very much like a zebra.

In 1772, the queen gave her 'ass' to an employee which ultimately led to the zebra going on a tour of the country. Beginning at Brentford, the zebra travelled on to Windsor, Reading and Oxford and finally became part of John Pinchbeck's menagerie, where she was last heard of early in 1774.

Clearly, imitation is the sincerest form of flattery, as we learn from an account of the proceedings at the Chester Quarter Sessions. Abraham Mylock, a stranger to the city, was the plaintiff and John Salladine, a wealthy innkeeper and brewer of Chester, was the defendant.

Mylock was the owner of a little cream-coloured, undocked mare which had been most ingeniously painted, stained and streaked in such a manner that she became a beautiful facsimile of the queen's greatly-admired zebra. Having created the deception, Mylock toured around the country with her exhibiting her everywhere he could, including, unfortunately for him, the Midsummer Fair at Chester; a big mistake.

It transpired that the preceding April, a Mr Salladine had lost a mare, about the size of the one being exhibited. He asserted that the mare he had lost was a bay mare with a docked tail and that the curious creature belonged to him. Mylock was apprehended and brought before a magistrate, was kept for more than seven hours in custody and would have been committed to the Northgate gaol, but a reputable tradesman testified that they had seen Mylock with the zebra for more than two years at several great fairs. With this news, Mylock was discharged but the story did not end there. Mylock was so angry at this stain upon his character that he counter-sued and after a hearing of nearly seven hours in which several witnesses were called for each side, the jury found in favour of Mylock.

Chapter Nine

Lady Wilbrahammon

I f Sarah Wilson had turned to the stage instead of a life of crime she would possibly be remembered as one of the greatest actresses of her day, for Sarah had a talent not just for pretending to be someone else but for making people truly believe her deception.

Born around 1746, Sarah had a rudimentary education; she could read and write, albeit imperfectly, but was intelligent and well-informed. When little more than a child she was working in the kitchen of a grand house in Leicester Fields (now Leicester Square) which belonged to George Lewis Scott, Esq., a noted

A View of Leicester Square, London, after Thomas Bowles. (*Yale Center for British Art, Paul Mellon Collection*)

Prince George and Prince Edward Augustus, sons of Frederick, Prince of Wales, with their tutor, Dr Francis Ayscough, Richard Wilson. (*Yale Center for British Art, Paul Mellon Collection*)

mathematician who had been a childhood tutor to Frederick, Prince of Wales's children, including the future King George III. (The Prince of Wales predeceased his father, George II and so, when the king died in 1760, his 22-year-old grandson took the throne as George III.)

Short and slender with black hair, Sarah had a 'speck' covering her right eye (which she hid by excessive winking) and a stoop in her shoulders which made her appear slightly deformed. Despite this, she snared the son of a wealthy Surrey farmer and broom-maker in matrimony. On 17 December 1764, at the village of Frensham, Sarah married Thomas Boxall but did so under an assumed name: Sarah Charlotte Lewissearn Wilbrowson. With delusions of grandeur clearly already evident, Sarah's new surname was an exaggerated version of her own, while Lewissearn recalled the middle name of her former employer. Sarah had arrived at the farmer's door in search of a lodging and as she looked genteel he gladly took her in. Claiming to be a nobleman's daughter, forced from her home and in possession of a fortune, Sarah charmed the old man; she was sprightly and engaging and played the guitar to perfection. Old Mr Boxall believed her and the gullible farmer was not about to let an opportunity slip through his fingers. He agreed to the marriage between Sarah and his son, kitting the young couple out in fine clothes and mortgaging his small estate so they could travel to London where Sarah claimed she could procure a colonel's commission for her new husband. For ten days over the Christmas and New Year period they lodged at the Bear Inn in the Borough and the new Mrs Boxall went almost daily in a coach to the west end of town on the pretence of gaining the commission and her fortune until the money ran out and she left London and her husband, who had to sell his horse to cover his expenses and travel home on foot.

By the following Christmas, Sarah was in Coventry where people were only too ready to believe the tall tale told to them.

Sarah insisted she was Lady Wilbrahammon, a gentlewoman in distress hailing from Corby Castle in Cumbria. She name-checked friends and relations in high places and duped people who were sympathetic to her plight into advancing funds or credit, always with the promise of repayment or other favours when she came into the estate she claimed was hers when she reached the age of 21. Her story varied depending on to whom she told it: to some, she wove a tale of abandonment because she followed the Protestant faith against the wishes of her Roman Catholic father and to others she gave a sob story involving the Honourable Mr Irving, a parson who Sarah loved but who her family were against.

From Coventry, Sarah travelled northward using various aliases: Lady Viscountess or Baroness Wilbrahammon, the Countess of Normandy and Miss Mollineaux were just a few. Eventually, she came to the village of Great Budworth in Cheshire where, now shabbily dressed, she found a warm welcome at Crowton Hall, the home of Richard Frith and his young family. The Friths totally believed Sarah's story. They housed her, fed her and provided her with a fine set of new clothes, a light-coloured riding habit together with a white hat sporting a blue feather and a cockade with golden tassels, and Sarah promised that, when she came into her estates and fortune, she would make Richard Frith her steward. Her 'inheritance' necessitated her travelling further north to Kendal and then to London, journeys financed by the kindly Friths. In fact, the Friths were so far duped by Sarah that they asked her and her suitor, the Honourable Mr Irving, to stand as godparents to their newly-born daughter and created a lasting reminder of their folly when the girl was baptized as Sarah Charlotta Irving Frith, with proxy godparents standing in for Sarah and her beau who – as might be surmised – were unavoidably detained from attending.

By June, 'Lady Wilbrahammon' was back in Coventry, claiming to have married Mr Irving while she was in Great Budworth but she had 'mislaid' her husband

Baltimore from Federal Hill, William James Bennett. (*National Gallery of Art, Collection of Mr and Mrs Paul Mellon*)

and was in distress. She visited the Earl of Denbigh but aroused his suspicions and the earl enlisted Alderman Hewitt to unravel the mystery. Ordered to remain at the inn where she was lodging while Hewitt travelled to London to verify her story, Sarah – wisely – decamped immediately. Using money 'borrowed' from the landlord of the inn, she headed for Banbury in Oxfordshire. However, newspapers the length and breadth of the country now carried letters revealing her deception and her description was circulated: she was still wearing the riding habit and hat bought for her by Richard Frith.

Sarah evaded capture until September 1767 when she was arrested at Devizes in Wiltshire and judged to be a vagabond, cheat and impostress. At her hearing, she

Opposite: King George III, Allan Ramsay. (*The Indianapolis Museum of Art at Newfields*)

confessed to her real name: Sarah Wilson. The game was up. A few months later, Sarah stood trial at Westminster assizes for a fraud committed two years earlier in a shop kept by Mrs Davenport in the Haymarket and for this she was sentenced to seven years' transportation.

Landing in Baltimore, Maryland in 1771, Sarah was 'purchased' by Mr Devall of Bush Creek, Frederick County but – true to form – soon absconded, travelling to South Carolina where she called herself Princess Susanna Carolina Mathilda and claimed to be the sister of Queen Charlotte, duping the local gentry and promising them favours as she went in return for their hospitality.

It is not clear if Sarah was ever recaptured, although Mr Devall advertised for his runaway servant to be returned. It was rumoured that she married Captain William Henry Talbot of the 17th Regiment of Light Dragoons sometime after 1775 but as Captain Talbot – a bachelor who died in the US in 1782 – was the brother of the Honourable John Chetwynd-Talbot, 1st Earl Talbot, this can probably be laid to rest as the last tall tale in the life of Sarah Wilson.

Chapter Ten

The Queen of Smugglers

It is astonishing that such Numbers of our Ladies will subject themselves to high Penalties for wearing Chintz Gowns, when at an equal Expence they might be furnished with the elegant Silks of Spitalfields.

The Countess of Holderness was an unlikely criminal. Of Dutch extraction, Mary Doublet married Robert Darcy, the 4th Earl of Holderness in 1743 and bore him three children, two short-lived sons and a daughter, Lady Amelia Darcy. In their early married life the family lived abroad but, towards the end of July 1764, they arrived back in England complete with all their belongings. Unfortunately, Lord and Lady Holderness were stopped by customs officials in Dover and their extensive baggage was searched.

To protect the domestic textile manufacturers, and in particular the Spitalfields silk industry, it was illegal to import foreign silks. The bright and bold floral-patterned painted cottons or chintzes from India were also banned and could not be imported, sold or worn and, although these restrictions were widely flouted, the penalties – as Lady Holderness was about to discover – were harsh: fines could be levied and all the apparel deemed to be contraband seized.

There were more than 100 gowns in Lady Holderness's baggage and zealous customs officials discovered richly-embroidered and brocaded French and Italian wrought silk sacks and petticoats, Indian silks and chintzes (some already made into gowns and some cut and ready to be sewn), French alamode cloaks and much more. Lady Holderness was left with little more than the clothes in which she stood. Richly-embroidered waistcoats belonging to Lord Holderness were also taken and even the maids and servants' property did not escape notice. Yet to arrive at Dover was all the household furniture.

The couple's friends among the nobility were concerned, albeit mainly for their own illicit cargo which they too were in the habit of discreetly conveying from France to England. Lady Mary Coke wrote that 'since the seizure of Lord and Lady Holderness's baggage, everything that can be is taken from everybody', and in Lady Holland's opinion, 'Lady Holderness has done us all great mischief – indeed the officers are so exceeding strict just now, 'tis a bad time to attempt getting anything from abroad.'

Lady in a Pink Silk Dress, Allan Ramsay. (*Yale Center for British Art, Paul Mellon Collection*)

A View of the Castle and Town of Dover, James Mason after George Lambert. (*Yale Center for British Art, Paul Mellon Collection*)

Henceforth Lady Holderness became known as the 'Queen of Smugglers' but it did not curtail her activities. Four years later Lady Mary Coke was staying with her ladyship at Walmer Castle near to Deal in Kent (Lord Holderness held the position of Warden of the Cinque Ports and his wife used this as a cover to import contraband). On Friday, 17 June 1768, Lady Mary recorded in her diary that, after breakfast, the two ladies walked to Deal where Lady Holderness took her friend to the houses of three men who smuggled India goods, pretty silks, tea and muslin; the latter, to Lady Mary's delight, available at around half the price one would expect to pay in London.

Lady Holderness's escapades were still being talked about in 1769 when Horace Walpole wrote from Paris to his friend George Montagu to complain that since her ladyship had 'invaded the customs house with a hundred and fourteen gowns… the ports are so guarded, that not a soul but a smuggler can smuggle anything into England'.

None of her somewhat shady activities hindered Lady Holderness socially; in fact, they probably enhanced her status as she became a trusted source for the fabrics and gowns so craved by the ladies of the court. In 1770, she was appointed Lady of the Bedchamber to Queen Charlotte, wife of King George III and, even though she held this high-ranking position, Lady Holderness still dared to smuggle goods from France to England.

Sophia Charlotte, Princess of Mecklenburg-Strelitz, Queen of England, Georg David Matthieu. (*Nationalmuseum Sweden*)

In the autumn of 1778, Lady Holderness was once again thwarted by the revenue officers of the Custom House:

> A superb court dress, belonging to a lady of quality, has just been seized by some of the revenue officers and carried to the Custom House. The elegance of the dress draws a number of spectators to behold it. It is a white spotted sattin [*sic*] ground, embroidered with gold, white, pearls, and foiles of various colours. Other pieces of silk, black and white crape, trimmings, gloves, &c. to a large amount, were likewise seized in the same chest. The principal piece of silk is said to have been intended as a court dress for her Ladyship's daughter.

Truly, Lady Holderness was the Queen of Smugglers!

Chapter Eleven

Circumnavigating Sir Joseph Banks' Women

Sir Joseph Banks' achievements are well-known. Born in 1743 to William Banks of Revesby Abbey, he is arguably Lincolnshire's most famous son. Circumnavigating the globe, Banks was a renowned and eminent botanist and naturalist, but less well-known are the details of his private life as a young man.

Educated at Harrow, Eton and then at Christ Church, University of Oxford where the city 'echoed with his amours, and the bed-makers of [Christ Church] college have given the world some testimonials of his vigour' (Banks left without a degree), in 1763 he relocated to Chelsea where his widowed mother had taken Turret House on Paradise Row by the Chelsea Physic Garden. A year later, aged just 21, Joseph Banks inherited Revesby Abbey.

Banks' interest in botany stemmed from his schooldays and he now had leisure to indulge his passion: frequently found at the Physic Garden, Banks cultivated the plants and useful contacts in equal measure. With his prestige growing, Banks found himself in demand: he was elected to the Royal Society, advised George III on supporting voyages of discovery and began to sail on such expeditions. Between 1768 and 1771 Banks sailed to the Pacific Ocean on HMS *Endeavour* together with Captain James Cook.

He left behind a young woman named Julia Henrietta 'Harriet' Blossett, the ward of James Lee of the Vineyard Nursery in Hammersmith (a Scottish gardener who had once been an apprentice at the Chelsea Physic Garden). Harriet believed the handsome young botanist would claim her hand in marriage, but Banks returned a very different man from the one who had sailed away three years earlier. In Tahiti, where *Endeavour* moored for three months while the scientific men on board observed the transit of Venus across the sun, Banks, like many men on the voyage, took a Tahitian woman as a lover and fully embraced their culture, even getting tattooed. The Tahitians had a much more relaxed attitude towards sex and relationships compared to the taboos prevalent back home, and Harriet no longer held charms for him. Plus, Banks was now famous and his company sought after by London society; the restriction of a marriage was the last thing he wanted. The engagement to Harriet was broken, Banks writing to tell her that he loved her but was too volatile to marry. An interview followed, lasting 'from ten o'clock at night to ten the next morning' but to no avail, although a bargain was struck. Reneging on his promise cost Banks £5,000 in compensation.

Sir Joseph Banks, Joyce Aris after Sir Joshua Reynolds. (*Museum of New Zealand, Te Papa Tongarewa*)

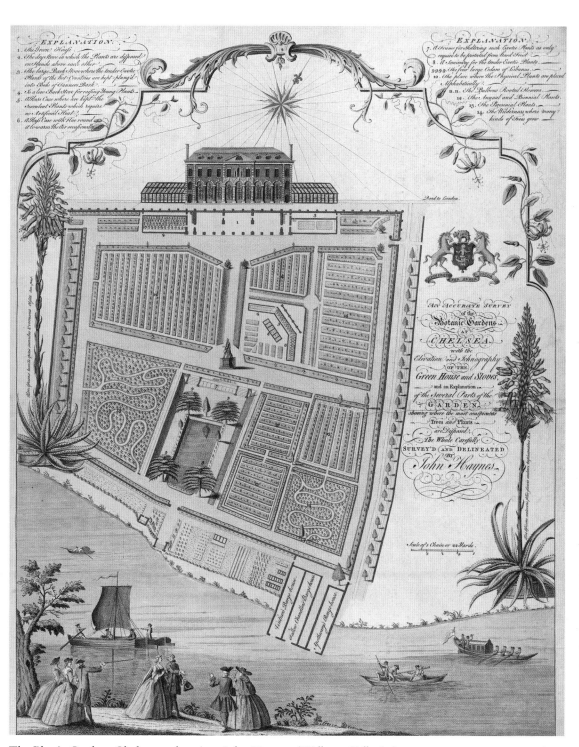

The Physic Garden, Chelsea: a plan view, John Haynes. (*Wellcome Collection*)

Plate from 'Histories of the tête-à-tête annexed'. (Town and Country Magazine (*1773*))

Banks' attention was soon directed elsewhere, however. Before setting sail and while residing in Chelsea, he had frequently spent time with a spirited, intelligent and pretty young girl who was a pupil at Blacklands House boarding school on Chelsea Common, just north of the King's Road. (Thomas Gainsborough's two daughters Molly and Peggy were pupils there. The same age as Banks' young friend, did they know of the burgeoning friendship between the botanist and the schoolgirl?) At the age of 17 and just before Banks had sailed from England, she left the school; her name is lost to history and she is recorded merely as Miss B__n.

With Harriet out of the way, Banks began to ask after Miss B__n and when he found her, he discovered that she was in reduced circumstances. Her father, a gentleman of fortune, had died while Banks had been away; he had gambled away everything he owned and left his daughter with nothing. To survive, she had taken the position of companion to an old lady, living in her house and totally reliant on her largesse, but it was a dull existence and one that denied the amorous botanist the chance to properly renew their acquaintance. He stepped

Matavai Bay, Tahiti, William Hodges. (*Yale Center for British Art, Paul Mellon Collection*)

in and found Miss B__n lodgings with a decent family where he could visit, his intention clear although, when he chaperoned her to parties and on days out, it was always in the company of another young lady who boarded in the same house. The strict rules of decency were closely adhered to. Until, that is, the companion was taken ill and unable to accompany Banks and Miss B__n on a planned jaunt to Hampton Court: the pair went anyway and, as their friendship had turned to love, nature took its course. It was soon all too obvious that Miss B__n had given in to her desires and Banks set her up in a finely-furnished house on Orchard Street where, in the autumn of 1773, she gave birth to Banks' child. The pair tried – and to a surprising degree were successful – to avoid gossip. The only references to their love affair are a letter dated November 1773 from Banks' friend, the Danish zoologist Johan Christian Fabricius, enquiring about the baby and a gossipy *tête-à-tête* in the September edition of the *Town and Country* magazine for the same year which noted that the couple were mutually fond of their child and that the new arrival had 'still farther increased their affection and regard' for each other. Miss B__n's neighbours and even her servants believed her to be married but she was not, although 'in everything except the ceremony, there [was] scarce the most trivial distinction'.

Who then was the woman waiting to be smuggled aboard the *Resolution* disguised as Banks' male valet at Madeira in the summer of 1772? Captain Cook was leading a second voyage of discovery and Joseph Banks had initially planned to be a part of the expedition but was withdrawn at the last minute. The 'valet' was introduced to Cook as Mr Burnett, who had left London at about the time the *Resolution* was first ready to sail and who had been waiting in Madeira for three months for the ship to arrive. In a letter, Cook said that

> at first he [Burnett] said he came here for the recovery of his health, but afterwards said his intention was to go out with Mr Banks, to some he said he was unknown to this Gentleman, to others he said it was by his appointment he came here as he could not be received on board in England, at last when he heard that Mr Banks did not go, he took the very first opportunity to get off the Island, he was about 30 years of age, and rather ordinary than otherwise and employ'd his time in Botanizing &c – every part of Mr Burnett's behaviour and every action tended to prove he was a Woman, I have not met with a person that entertains a doubt of contrary nature.

Nothing further is known about Miss B__n or 'Mr Burnett' and within a year or two Banks had a new mistress, Sarah Wells. In 1776, Banks and his mentor John Montagu, 4th Earl of Sandwich – who was associated with the notorious Hellfire Club (and was the inventor of the humble sandwich) – took a fishing trip together. Also in the party were Lord Mulgrave and 'two or three Ladies of pleasure', possibly Sarah and Sandwich's long-term mistress, the singer Martha Ray (who would be murdered outside the theatre in Covent Garden three years later by an obsessed stalker). Sarah Wells presided at Banks' table, was introduced to all his friends and the pair lived happily together for some years until parting amicably when Banks married an heiress, Dorothea Hugessen in March 1779. Two years later, Dorothea gained the title Lady Banks when her husband was made a baronet. It proved a happy, if childless union and Banks was a faithful and devoted husband.

Opposite: Captain James Cook, John Webber. (*Museum of New Zealand, Te Papa Tongarewa*)

Elizabeth Hartley as Hermione
in *The Winter's Tale*, Angelica
Kauffman. (*The Garrick Club*)

Chapter Twelve

Mrs Hartley and the 'Impudent Puppies'

Mrs Hartley was a striking red-headed beauty with a lively disposition. She was made for the stage, even though she disparagingly said of herself that: 'Nay, my face may be well enough for shape, but sure 'tis freckled as a toad's belly.'

Mrs Hartley was an assumed name; she was really Elizabeth White, born in the small village of Berrow in Somerset, the daughter of James and Eleanor White who 'occupied a position of great obscurity'.

Sir Joshua Reynolds painted Elizabeth's portrait when she was living with a bawd named Mrs Kelly in Little James Street, Haymarket in 1771 (Kelly later moved upmarket to Arlington St, Piccadilly where she opened a brothel in which Emma Hart, later Lady Hamilton, was one of her girls), but Elizabeth preferred it to be known that she worked as a chambermaid in a 'gentleman's house'. Whosoever owned the house, gentleman or bawd, Elizabeth fell for the charms of a handsome young man visiting the establishment and quit her position to run away with him. To avoid detection and the displeasure of his friends, it is said that he assumed Hartley as a surname and so too did Elizabeth.

Mr Hartley's meagre funds were soon depleted and he persuaded Elizabeth to take to the stage and provide an income. To be fair, she needed little encouragement and in no time was treading the boards in Edinburgh and then in Bristol, to varying reviews.

David Garrick took an interest, thinking of bringing Elizabeth to Drury Lane. Despite the fact that Mrs Hartley had already been snapped up by the rival Covent Garden theatre, the actor John Moody reported back to Garrick's brother George with an appraisal of the actress:

> Mrs Hartley is a good figure, with a handsome small face, and very much freckled; her hair red and her neck and shoulders well turned. There is not the least harmony in her voice; but when forced (which she never fails to do on every occasion) is loud and strong, but such an inarticulate gabble, that you must be acquainted with her part to understand her. She is ignorant and stubborn: the latter might be got the better of at Drury Lane, and the former mended; but I despair of either at Covent Garden, where she is engaged: notwithstanding,

there is a superficial glare about her that may carry her through a few nights; but, be assured, she cannot last long. She has a husband, a precious fool, that she heartily despises. She talks lusciously, and has a slovenly good-nature about her that renders her prodigiously vulgar… This, Sir, is my real opinion of her, and yet I wish we had her; because I am sure she would do for Mr. Garrick that [which] no other man in the world will ever get her to think of, she is so stubborn.

Oh dear! Still, by the start of 1773 Elizabeth was renowned as 'the celebrated Mrs Hartley of the Covent Garden theatre.'

On a balmy summer evening, Mrs Hartley was seated on a bench in the illuminated groves of Vauxhall Gardens with her husband, a Mr Colman and the Reverend Henry Bate (later Sir Henry Bate Dudley, 1st Baronet), henceforth to be known as the Fighting Parson, an 'able and witty, but profligate man'. Bate was

Vaux-Hall, Thomas Rowlandson. (*Lewis Walpole Library, Yale University*)

involved with both the *Morning Post* and *Morning Herald* newspapers and would later write scripts for comic operas; in 1780 he married Elizabeth's equally red-haired sister, Mary White, but that did not prevent him from being named as the defendant in a Criminal Conversation case. (The law at the time viewed a married woman as part of the property or goods of her husband, hence Crim. Con. saw the husband suing for compensation due to the loss of his 'property' rights. Bate was accused of an affair with a Mrs Dodwell who had visited him for 'musical evenings' while he was held in the King's Bench Prison for libelling the Duke of Richmond. Reputedly, Mary passed Mrs Dodwell on the stairs of the prison one evening and gave the lady a piece of her mind.)

In Vauxhall, Elizabeth's beauty attracted the attention of four fashionable but louche macaronis seated at a table opposite, who professed themselves her 'admirers' and stared rudely, to Bate's anger. He deliberately placed himself in front of Mrs Hartley to hide her from view. Mrs Hartley rose to walk away, followed by the gentlemen of her party and there the matter may have ended but Mr Bate, as he left, loudly remarked that the men were 'four dirty, impudent puppies'. One of them, a Captain Crofts, followed Bate to forcibly protest the insult. On promenading around the gardens before leaving, Mrs Hartley and Bate encountered their foes once more. This time Bate was accosted by George Robert Fitzgerald, a 'little effeminate being' who was outraged on behalf of his friend, Captain Crofts. From a well-connected Irish family, Fighting Fitzgerald, as he was known, fought at least eighteen duels during his life and eventually ended his days on the gallows, convicted of murder.

The next morning, Captain Crofts issued a challenge to Bate. A meeting was arranged in the Turk's Head Coffee House where Crofts arrived accompanied by another friend, the 'wicked' Lord Lyttelton, Thomas, 2nd Baron Lyttelton. The dissolute Lyttelton enjoyed a reputation as both a libertine and a politician. He had married a wealthy East India Company (EIC) official's widow the preceding summer, mainly for the £20,000 she brought to the union and, following the ceremony, left his new bride in the lurch and decamped to Paris with a barmaid who had caught his eye. Ostensibly the rendezvous in the Coffee House was to demand an apology from Bate but really it was to corner him with Fitzgerald's footman, a prize-fighter who was falsely introduced as Fitzgerald's friend, Captain Miles. Bate, not easily frightened and confident in his own pugilistic abilities, calmly thrashed the captain so comprehensively that the man had to be taken away in a hackney cab, almost unconscious and with his face 'a perfect jelly'. Lord Lyttelton, to show there were no hard feelings, invited Mr Bate to dine with him the next day.

Bate was furious when he realized that Captain Miles was not an officer and a gentleman, but a lowly servant who was handy with his fists and he disputed with

Rev. Sir Henry Bate Dudley, Gainsborough Dupont. (*Yale Center for British Art, Paul Mellon Collection*)

the 'impertinent meddling puppy' Fitzgerald in a very public manner through a series of letters to the newspapers. In the end, 'the superior wit and powerful satire of Parson Bate were so manifest, that his opponents were beaten out of the literary arena.'

The publicity only served to increase Mrs Hartley's fame and she continued to tread the boards both at Covent Garden and at theatres in Ireland for several years. In 1774, while playing the role of the Fair Rosamund (the Rose of the World) in Henry II, she eloped to France with the actor who was playing her onstage lover. William 'Gentleman' Smith, a tall, handsome and well-educated merchant's son-turned-actor, was some twenty years Elizabeth's senior. Twenty years earlier, he had married the well-connected Elizabeth Courtenay, the 4th Earl of Sandwich's sister and widow of Kelland Courtenay of Powderham Castle in Devon and, after that lady's death, had wasted little time in snaring another heiress, Martha Newsom of Leiston in Suffolk. A purported letter from Smith to his long-suffering second wife, written at Dover as he left for France, was circulated at the time of his elopement:

> 27 May 1774
>
> My dear love – You and I have long lived happy together, and be assured at this very moment I love you more than any woman in the world. When you hear of the little excursions I am going to make with Mrs H___, be not alarmed; it is a sudden impulse of passion which I own I have not had the courage to resist. There is something so bewitching and enchanting in beauty, that it baffles our strongest resolutions; but it is an infatuation that will soon be over. You must pardon me this one slip, and believe me when I declare, that though a momentary gust of passion may hurry me into trifling indiscretions, I never can find real felicity and true happiness but in your arms.

Gentleman Smith's letters written a short time later from Dublin tell a different story, however. Seeking employment with David Garrick at Drury Lane, he was open about his love of his Fair Rosamund:

> 26 June 1774
>
> [Mrs Hartley] is determined (at all events) not to return to Covent-Garden, and I (at all events) am determined to be with her. I am in love and pleased with ruin. Cold complexions may talk of keeping amours secret, but who, when in love with, and beloved by such a woman, can live a moment from her... In plain terms: will you engage the Hartley and me this ensuing season or the succeeding one? We had as lieve stay here next year, but shall be happy to join you after it (or this, if you like better); and whatever I may be, she will be worth your bidding

for, I am sure. It is my wish and my pride to be with you, but I will not leave my Rose for the world… a pretty parcel of d__d lies in your papers, I see. Letters from Dover, &c. Mrs Smith is with her father, and writes to me as if she knew nothing of the matter.

Mrs Hartley, it seemed, had been in need of a 'protector' and Gentleman Smith had stepped up willingly to the role: Garrick engaged Smith to play at Drury Lane while Mrs Hartley returned to Covent Garden, and their affair was still going strong in the spring of 1775.

By the late 1770s, Elizabeth Hartley was in poor health and retired from the stage in 1780, moving to France and reverting to her former surname, White. She lived quietly and comfortably but privately for the remainder of her days, dying at her house in King Street (now the southern sweep of Kingsman Street), a short distance from the Dock Yard in Woolwich on 26 January 1824 at the age of 73.

A View of His Majesty's Dock Yard at Woolwich, Carington Bowles after John Cleveley the younger. (*Yale Center for British Art, Paul Mellon Collection*)

Chapter Thirteen

Emily Warren, an 'infamous and notoriously abandoned woman'

*E*mily Warren was born c.1760 in the slums of London and, until she was 12 years old, earned her living by leading her father – a blind beggar – by the hand around the streets of the capital, charming passers-by into dropping coins into their begging bowl. Eventually, the pretty urchin came to the attention of one of London's most notorious but successful brothel-keepers, Charlotte Hayes.

Charlotte recognized a prize when she saw one and was struck by Emily's youthful beauty; she enticed the girl into her 'house of delights' in King's Place, St James's. There, Emily was taught how to walk and talk like a lady and by 1776 was becoming a favourite with the patrons of the King's Place *nunnery*.

It is often said that beauty can be but skin deep and, if the memoirist William Hickey – who first met Emily in the King's Place brothel – is to be believed, this was all too apt a description. Stunningly beautiful with a well-formed figure and a lively and winning personality, Emily was also cold and unfeeling. Warren was probably not her real name; at various times Emily also used Bertie and Coventry, possibly all three surnames hinting at men who 'took her into keeping'. It was around this time that Charles Francis Greville, collector and MP, took an interest in Emily and introduced her to the painter Sir Joshua Reynolds, who depicted the young beauty as Thaïs, a courtesan who persuaded Alexander the Great to burn Persepolis. That great gossip, Horace Walpole, gleefully related that the portrait 'was drawn from a woman of the town, Emily Bertie, and is too masculine'. Greville couldn't pay for the painting (it ended up with Lord Dysart until Greville managed to reclaim it thirty years later) and perhaps Emily turned her attention to more lucrative beaux for her amour with Greville soon fizzled out. (Greville was later to become temporarily besotted with another of Charlotte Hayes' protégés, Emma Hart, who he introduced to George Romney much in the same way that he had introduced Emily to Reynolds; Emma Hart would go on to captivate Vice Admiral Horatio Lord Nelson and be bettered remembered to history as Emma, Lady Hamilton.)

Portrait of a Woman, said to be Emily Bertie Pott, George Romney. (*Metropolitan Museum of Art*)

Sir Joshua Reynolds, Thomas Peat. (*Metropolitan Museum of Art*)

William Hickey was also a close friend of Emily's final – and longest-lasting – protector, Robert Percival Pott who, like Hickey, was employed by the EIC's Civil Service. Robert Pott arrived back in London in August of 1778 and made the acquaintance of Emily soon after. In no time at all, she was openly living with him and calling herself Mrs Pott.

When Hickey arrived in London two years later, he was almost instantly accosted by Emily, resplendently dressed in the latest fashions and seated in a splendid yellow *vis-à-vis* with the Pott arms on the doors. She had been sent by Robert who had just left for Portsmouth and a berth on a ship heading for Bengal. He had been thwarted in his plans to take his mistress with him, the two even planning to disguise Emily as a boy and passing her off as Pott's manservant to get her aboard. Instead, she was ensconced in a fine fully-furnished house on Cork Street in Mayfair on which Pott had paid the rent for fifteen months in advance; Robert wished his friend Hickey to take care of Emily. Hickey, in his memoirs, stressed that Emily placed her *vis-à-vis* and carriage (both newly-purchased from Hatchet of Long Acre), her servants, house and all it contained at his disposal; when Emily eagerly invited him into her bedroom, Hickey delightedly accepted.

He was a rake who had form for sleeping with his friends' mistresses. Hickey fell head over heels in love with Charlotte Barry, a courtesan who was 'in the keeping of' the Earl of Peterborough's elder – and illegitimate – brother, Henry Mordaunt, also an officer in the EIC's army, and happily entertained Charlotte while Mordaunt picked up the bills. (The infamous courtesan Grace Dalrymple Elliott was the Mordaunt brothers' cousin; this louche and lax society was all too tightly-knit.)

Robert Pott never made it to Bengal, for his ship was among several captured by the Spanish and he was taken prisoner and held in Madrid from where he wrote to sing the praises of the señoritas he had met, to Emily's disapproval. As soon as he was released, Robert headed back to Emily's forgiving arms, all the more forgiving as George Romney was commissioned to paint portraits of the pair.

India still beckoned and when he recommenced his voyage, Robert was able to gain permission for Emily to sail with him to Bengal aboard the *Lord Mulgrave*, an Indiaman under Captain James Urmston. A last-ditch attempt to thwart Emily embarking was made by Percivall Pott, Robert's father, who thought her an 'infamous and notoriously abandoned woman … who had already involved him deeply as to pecuniary matters.' He believed her presence in India would shut his son out of proper society and ruin Robert's prospects of employment, but it was to no avail. Robert Pott and Emily left the shores of England and sailed to India, landing first at Madras where they remained for a while. Emily charmed everyone: 'The men universally declared they had never beheld so beautiful a creature as Emily, and even the women admitted her extraordinary beauty of face and person.'

Portrait of a Gentleman, possibly William Hickey, and an Indian Servant, Arthur William Devis. (*Yale Center for British Art, Paul Mellon Collection*)

In May 1782, Robert and Emily left Madras bound for Kolkata. The weather was humid and, although otherwise fit and healthy, Emily was suffering badly from 'prickly heat', a rash which made her skin sensitive and was a common affliction for newcomers to India. Drinking cold fluids provided relief from the discomfort but usually worsened the rash; however, Emily was hot and heedless. She drank two tumblers of cold milk diluted with water, one after the other, and almost immediately her vision blurred and she felt faint. Sitting down, she fell unconscious and died, her vivacious life shockingly snuffed out in a matter of minutes.

Emily's body was put in a hastily-found coffin, placed in a small boat and towed behind the ship to Kolkata where she was buried. Robert Pott enlisted Mr Tiretta, an Italian resident in India, to build a mausoleum over her grave and also to erect a

Calcutta (now Kolkata), Samuel Davis. (*Yale Center for British Art, Paul Mellon Collection*)

column 'amongst herds of tigers' close to the Diamond Harbour at Kulpi, off the shore of which Emily had died. This latter was known as Pott's Folly.

NB: Robert Pott remained in India, marrying his wealthy cousin Sarah Cruttenden in 1788 and dying in 1795.

Chapter Fourteen

The Astronomer William Herschel and his Sister Caroline, a 'Heavenly Hausfrau'

The Herschels were a Hanoverian family, several members of whom settled in England (the House of Hanover remained united with England throughout the Georgian era). Sir William Herschel (born 1738) is best remembered as an astronomer – he discovered the planet Uranus – but was also a talented musician and symphonic composer, and a skilled linguist.

Caroline Lucretia Herschel, William's sister (born 1750, the second youngest of the family), was denied the education given to her brothers and instead 'kept house' for her illiterate and domineering widowed mother in Germany, living a life of downtrodden drudgery and desperate to see the world her brothers inhabited. Small in stature, the result of contracting typhus at the age of 11, Caroline's face was scarred following a bout of smallpox as a child. She remembered her father with fondness and – despite her lack of knowledge – he was responsible for opening her mind to the wonders of the universe. Memorably, Isaac Herschel took his young daughter outside on a cold and frosty but clear evening to acquaint her 'with the most beautiful constellations, after we had been gazing at a comet which was then visible', and Caroline remembered viewing an eclipse of the sun from a reflection in a bucket of water.

At last, in 1772, Caroline got her chance to escape her mother when William brought her to live with him in Bath, where he was pursuing a musical career (he had to pay his mother an annual sum to enable her to employ a substitute servant to replace her daughter). In Bath, Caroline's education began in earnest: William taught her to speak English as well as instructing her in mathematics and also gave her singing lessons. It had been the shy Caroline's ambition to become a concert singer, a secret she shared with no-one except her beloved brother. He was able to make her dreams reality and soon Caroline was appearing at musical entertainments in and around Bath. William, an amateur astronomer, also gave his sister a rudimentary telescope and reflector, introducing her to the music of the spheres.

Her education continued apace and, as William slowly became interested more in astronomy than music, Caroline learned at his side, working as his star-gazing assistant. Initially, she was little more than a housekeeper, bringing her brother drinks and food, almost hand-feeding him as he obsessively immersed himself in his studies, but in time she began to assist in polishing and grinding the mirrors used in his home-made telescopes, a long and arduous task. William pioneered the use of reflectors which increased magnification and light-gathering, rather than refractors. Their elegant Bath town house was turned into a busy, chaotic workshop which Caroline tried in vain to keep tidy. In addition to this, William established a small millinery business in his basement, an enterprise run by Caroline to supplement their income.

In 1781, William Herschel, with his ever-patient and industrious sister by his side, discovered a new planet, one which had been noticed before but always mistaken for a star (William initially thought it a comet). The scientific world was amazed and impressed in equal measure: this was the first planet to be discovered since the days of pre-history and even the Royal Astronomer, Nevil Maskelyne, thought the heavens were already thoroughly mapped out. Nobody had been searching for a new planet... except for the Herschels who could see further than anyone else

Sir William Herschel exhibiting his 20ft telescope to George III at Datchet or Clay Hall, John Inigo Richards. (*Lewis Walpole Library, Yale University*)

On the Road to Datchet, after Thomas Sandby. (*Yale Center for British Art, Paul Mellon Collection*)

with their innovative 7ft telescope. George III appointed William as his personal astronomer with a handsome salary, allowing him to give up his musical career to concentrate full time on astronomy ('Herschel should not sacrifice his valuable time to crotchets and quavers,' said the king).

In honour of the king, and with the agreement of Sir Joseph Banks, President of the Royal Society, William named his discovery 'the Georgium Sidus' (the Georgian Planet) but this was soon vetoed and changed to one from classic mythology to conform with the other planetary names: Uranus was chosen, the name of the Greek god of the heavens.

A relocation to the village of Datchet near Slough and – more importantly – Windsor Castle took place the following year. William had promised Caroline that one day she would be an independent woman, earning a living as a successful concert singer; however, Caroline sacrificed her dream to move to the quiet backwater that was Datchet and help her brother achieve his ambition. The royal family were frequent visitors, observing the heavens through a newly-built 20ft telescope in the grounds of the Herschels' home, a wing of a substantial house known as The Lawns.

At Datchet, as well as running the household, Caroline was officially named William's assistant astronomer, a 'Heavenly Hausfrau' who swept the night skies for comets with her own telescope. Dressed in layers of woollen petticoats to keep warm, initially she hated spending cold dark nights outside observing the skies, but once she had more specialized equipment she began to discover comets herself and to enjoy her new career, even if she did find Datchet remote after the bustling life

Herschel's 40ft Telescope at Slough. (ETH-Bibliothek Zürich, Bildarchiv/Fotograf: Unbekannt/ Ans_03780/Public Domain Mark).

she had enjoyed in Bath. Still, a steady flow of interested visitors made their way to the observatory at Datchet.

Four years later, the Herschels moved to Clay Hall in Old Windsor and then to The Grove at Slough (later known as Observatory House) where a giant 40ft telescope was built. It was so enormous that people could walk through during its construction. When George III visited with the Archbishop of Canterbury and the prelate faltered, the king turned around, took his hand, and exclaimed, 'Come, my Lord Bishop, I will show you the way to Heaven!'

The Meteor of August 18, 1783, as seen from the East Angle of the North Terrace, Windsor Castle, Paul Sandby. (*Yale Center for British Art, Paul Mellon Collection*)

Eight comets and several nebulae were detected by Caroline – the first female comet-hunter – and, in 1787 she received a pension of her own from the royal purse plus the distinction of being the first woman ever to be granted one for scientific work. Sir Joseph Banks suggested that the pension should come from Queen Charlotte rather than George III as Caroline was 'the lady's comet hunter'. It is perhaps noteworthy that all of her discoveries were made when her brother was otherwise occupied or away from home.

Despite becoming an astronomer in her own right (she once rode through the night to Greenwich to announce her discovery of a comet to Maskelyne rather than risk someone else claiming it), Caroline remained her brother's assistant in his own celestial observations. She would sit, sometimes until dawn and with paper and ink beside her, to await a signal from William, viewing the heavens through his telescope, who would then shout out information for Caroline to record. From these scribbled notes, the next day she would write up her brother's observations.

The partnership between brother and sister was disrupted in 1788 when William married a neighbouring widow and Caroline moved out of her home into a cottage nearby. From an observation platform on its roof, Caroline still swept the night skies and she continued to assist her brother, although her enthusiasm waned for a time.

Caroline returned to Hanover after William's death in 1822 and catalogued her brother's work (Caroline lived to be 97). The astronomical observations and calculations of the Herschels revolutionized the way people perceived the solar system, the Milky Way galaxy and the whole meaning and structure of the universe. While William had initially taken the lead in their discoveries, subsequently Caroline had been the driving force behind his impetus. As William himself admitted, 'it was not always self-evident which was the planet, and which was the moon.'

Queen Charlotte, Benjamin West. (*Yale Center for British Art, Paul Mellon Collection*)

Mrs Crouch, George Romney. (*Philadelphia Museum of Art, The John Howard McFadden Collection, M1928-1-31*)

Chapter Fifteen

The Fabulously Famous Anna Maria Crouch

Anna Maria, known to her family as Nancy, was baptized on 10 May 1762 at St Andrew, Holborn, not 1763 as recorded in her memoirs (a lady never tells her true age, now does she?). She was one of the six children of Peregrine Phillips and his wife Mary who lived on Gray's Inn Lane (now Gray's Inn Road), London. Peregrine was an attorney by profession and something of a writer and poet whose works received mixed reviews. He was also a close

An Audience Watching a Play at Drury Lane Theatre, Thomas Rowlandson. (*Yale Center for British Art, Paul Mellon Collection*)

friend of Drs Benjamin Franklin and Samuel Johnson. There were fanciful claims that through his mother, Peregrine had familial links to Charlotte Corday, a Frenchwoman who had assassinated the radical politician Jean-Paul Marat in 1793 during the French Revolution (Corday stabbed Marat while he was in his bathtub; she was later guillotined for her crime).

Just before Anna's 13th birthday her mother died, leaving Peregrine to raise their children unaided. Realizing that Anna was both talented and beautiful with a sweet (although not powerful) voice like a 'silver bell', Peregrine began his quest to transform Anna into the famous actress and opera singer she ultimately became, and one of the most renowned talents of her day.

Anna's reputation as a singer grew and in 1779 she was contracted for three years to the composer Mr Linley, the father of Elizabeth Linley, wife of playwright Richard Brinsley Sheridan. Late in 1780, she made her debut as Xerxes' daughter Mandane, alongside the acclaimed Sophia Baddeley, in Thomas Arne's opera *Artaxerxes*. The newspapers acknowledged it was her first performance and were not overly unkind, putting her less than average performance down to nerves and remarking that 'her blemishes seemed to arise more from a lack of musical education than from nature.'

In 1783, Anna Maria and her father, with a letter of recommendation from Dr Samuel Johnson, travelled to Dublin where one of the most famous actors of the era, John Philip Kemble, was playing at Smock Alley Theatre.

Anna, by this time, was much in demand not only in terms of employment but also by suitors. One rejected swain was so frantic for her hand in marriage that he threatened to shoot her if she did not accept his offer. When she spied him sitting in the audience, Anna refused to go on stage.

A Mr Loftus from a well-connected Irish family was more successful in his advances and Anna agreed to be his wife. The couple fled to Gretna Green, but Mr Phillips was not about to lose the valuable asset he owned in his talented daughter and they were caught before they reached the famous blacksmith's shop. The bride-to-be was returned to her father in London where she continued to perform at Drury Lane and took on her most challenging role, Polly Peachum in *The Beggar's Opera*. It was proclaimed a massive hit by the press and, with this, she secured her future. Her 'habitual defects' and stage fright conquered, Anna became the highest-paid actress of the day. Her name appeared in the press almost daily until, on 9 January 1785, there was a different report.

> Miss Phillips, of Drury Lane Theatre, married a young gentleman of Manchester.

That young gentleman was a naval lieutenant named Rollings Edward Crouch and the couple had tied the knot at Twickenham. By all accounts, their marriage got

George, Prince of Wales, English School. (*Royal Pavilion & Museums, Brighton & Hove* (*CC BY-SA*))

The Thames at Twickenham, Samuel Scott. (*Yale Center for British Art, Paul Mellon Collection*)

off to a good start and Anna soon found herself pregnant but, tragically, she gave birth a month prematurely and the baby, a daughter, died within two days.

Anna, now billed as Mrs Crouch, continued to act and her husband joined her on her travels around the country. However, some eighteen months into the marriage rumours began to spread that the couple were going to India and that there was disharmony between them. According to the artist Joseph Farrington, the Prince of Wales (later George IV) was smitten with Anna, a state of affairs that resulted in the lady receiving a settlement of £1,200, presumably for services rendered. Her husband received a smaller amount to deter him from bringing an action against the prince.

In 1787 Crouch paid George Romney, the fashionable portrait painter of the day, to paint his wife's portrait while she was dressed in the character Adelaide from the *Count of Narbonne*, but if this was an attempt to regain Anna's affections it failed to work. She packed her bags and left for Dublin with the actor and singer Michael Kelly, a move which saw the start of more than just a professional relationship. Rumours were to abound of a *ménage à trois* which appears to have lasted several years. Ultimately, Crouch left Anna.

While Anna and Kelly lived harmoniously together, Crouch reappeared in Salisbury, Wiltshire where he committed bigamy by marrying a wealthy young woman named Catherine Rider in 1795. No longer a lieutenant in the navy, he

Anna Maria Crouch as Polly Peachum in *The Beggar's Opera* by John Gay. (*The Garrick Club*)

was now serving in the army as a cornet in the 12th Regiment of Dragoons and he changed his name slightly from Rollings to Rowland and Crouch to Couch to obfuscate detection of his crime. Despite this, Catherine's relatives soon discovered that the marriage was bigamous, and they sought redress from the law. Anna was contacted and asked about her marriage but, still clearly on reasonable terms with her husband, she forewarned him that questions were being asked, prompting Crouch to flee the country for a time. Once the fuss had died down he slipped back and lived quietly with Catherine, siring two sons by her and using Calvert as the family's surname. The elder of these sons, Edward, was born in the sleepy fishing village of Appledore in north Devon and would become a noted artist and engraver, counting the poet and painter William Blake among his close friends. Crouch, or Calvert as we suppose we must now refer to him, became the captain of the Bideford Yeomanry before taking up a similar position with the Devon Guides, stationed at Starcross, while his family moved to the small Cornish village of St Winnow on the banks of the River Fowey near Lostwithiel where he joined them shortly before his death in 1813 aged 50. In his will, written in 1809, he named himself as Rawlins Edward or Rollings Calvert, late Crouch and, for the avoidance of doubt, declared in that document that:

> I do hereby expressly declare my Will and intention to be that the said Catherine whether our marriage may have been strictly legal or not shall be absolutely intitled [*sic*] to the whole of my Estate and Effects to and for her own absolute use benefit and disposal.

Anna remained with Michael Kelly until her death in Brighton on 2 October 1805.

Chapter Sixteen

Up, Up and Away

Even today people are fascinated by watching hot air balloons gliding gracefully across a clear blue sky on a warm summer's day. Until the 1780s the idea of being able to fly in any form was a concept that could only be imagined. That was until the arrival of the Montgolfier brothers, Joseph-Michel and Jacques-Étienne; it was Jacques-Étienne who became the first ever person to 'fly' when he made a tethered flight in 1783, narrowly beating his countryman, Jean-François Pilâtre de Rozier who took to the skies later that same day, although the latter holds the claim to having made the first untethered flight later that year. Other early aeronautical pioneers included Jean-Pierre Blanchard and the Italian, Vincenzo Lunardi.

Everyone wanted to get in on the act and attempts were made on quite a regular basis, much to the delight of the crowds who assembled to watch. We are going to look at the first women who daringly took part in such flights.

It is a Frenchwoman who holds the distinction of being the first to ascend in an untethered balloon. In June 1784, 19-year-old opera singer Marie Élisabeth Thible from Lyons (the abandoned wife of a wealthy merchant), dressed as the Roman goddess Minerva, accompanied the painter Mr Fleurant in a Montgolfière balloon. The 'aerostatic nymph', as she was known, was a last-minute stand-in for Count Jean-Baptiste de Laurencin who could not summon up the courage to ascend (he had previously taken part in a flight that had ended badly). Understandably the crowds watching, which included Gustav III of Sweden for whom the balloon was named, and Louis XVI and his queen Marie Antoinette, were completely shocked to see a woman in the sky.

Later that same year, Jean-Pierre Blanchard entertained the guests of Monsieur and Madame Dudonet with tethered flights in his balloon from the grounds of their château. Several ladies were among those who bravely ascended to a height of 80ft including two who travelled together, the first all-female flight. Blanchard was very appreciative of the ladies' courage and enthusiasm, applauding their spirit and claiming that they would all make excellent companions on a difficult voyage.

On 15 September 1784, to the cheers of spectators who included the Prince of Wales, Vincenzo Lunardi, the 'Daredevil Aeronaut', took off from the Artillery Ground at Moorfields, London in what was to be the first manned free-floating balloon flight in England. Although he intended to take at least one passenger with

The First Balloon Ascent in England, September 1784, from the Artillery Ground, Moorfields, Francis Jukes after an unknown artist. (*Yale Center for British Art, Paul Mellon Collection*)

him, in the end the balloon would not inflate sufficiently and so he made do with a dog, a cat and a pigeon for company (the pigeon escaped, and the cat and dog were air-sick and were dispensed with on a descent at Welham Green).

Taking to the skies once again, Lunardi continued his flight until he made an unscheduled landing at Standon, near Ware, Hertfordshire. Elizabeth Brett was hard at work in Thomas Read's brew-house when a strange noise caught her attention. Peering out of the door, she saw 'a strange large body… a machine which she knew not what to make of' in the air; intrigued, Elizabeth went for a closer look. Lunardi called down to her, told her that it was an air balloon and asked that she would grab hold of a rope so that he could land. Elizabeth did as she was requested and held firm. Not so the two labouring men who also came for a look; one said he was too short and the other was too afraid, and both made their excuses. The plucky Elizabeth kept her grip on the rope, but it was not until some harvesters joined in that the balloon was brought in to land.

In England, though, it was to be a little while longer before a woman took to the skies. The famed Duchess of Devonshire was one of the spectators watching an ascent by Blanchard over London at the end of 1784 and she had the honour of signalling the start of the flight by releasing a small balloon and loosening the ropes that tethered Blanchard's balloon but at this stage, that was as far as a woman's participation in such an event was to go on this side of the Channel.

Georgiana, Duchess of Devonshire, Thomas Gainsborough. (*National Gallery of Art, Andrew W. Mellon Collection*)

That was all to change on a fine day in May 1785, when Mademoiselle Rosine Simonet, a slight young lady aged just 15 and weighing only 83lb, accompanied Blanchard on an aerial excursion from Mr Langhorne's Repository (where horses and carriages were bought and sold) in the Barbican area of London. Rosine, a Parisian by birth, was the daughter of Louis Simonet, dancer and ballet master, and the elder sister of Leonora (or Eleanor) and Theresa Simonet. All three sisters danced and sang on the London stages. When Mr Blanchard and his companion had taken their seats, the cords were cut and the balloon ascended. The day was still with little in the way of a breeze and so the spectators were entertained with several manoeuvres while it was completely in flight.

Mr Blanchard threw out some of the bags of ballast and the balloon headed off over Islington. They didn't ascend to any great height; in fact, they were so low that they were able to hear the huzzahs from the people on the ground below. After about half an hour they put down in a field adjacent to Lee Bridge turnpike, after which there was a triumphal procession through Clapton and Hackney back to the Barbican. According to the press of the day, Miss Simonet suffered from air-sickness and fainted several times. Horace Walpole wrote that 'a French girl, daughter of a dancer, has made a voyage into the clouds, and nobody has yet broken a neck; so, neither good nor harm has hitherto been produced by these aerial enterprises.' Monsieur Blanchard was clearly great friends with the Simonet family for, just over a fortnight after Rosine's ascent, he allowed her 13-year-old sister Leonora to accompany him on a second flight from the Barbican.

The first British woman to brave this new craze was Letitia Ann Sage, née Hoare, a London actress and dresser at the Drury Lane Theatre, aged 30, from an acting family and the common-law wife of a Cheapside haberdasher. Letitia made her maiden voyage on 30 June 1785. It was intended that Vincenzo Lunardi, an old Etonian named George Biggin who was Lunardi's sponsor and Mrs Sage would all take part in the aeronautical adventure which departed from St George's Fields in Newington. It took Lunardi three hours to inflate the Union Jack balloon to the point where he estimated it would be able to carry the three of them, but he miscalculated. Letitia alone apparently weighed some 200lb: she was a great deal heavier than the slim and svelte Miss Simonet. Lunardi – ever the gentleman – had neglected to ask the lady's weight. Mrs Sage, perhaps with some justification, has politely been referred to as 'Junoesque'. An earlier planned ascent with the three daring aeronauts had already failed to take to the skies, embarrassingly after an engraving of the three of them together in the basket of the balloon had been published.

The canopy, oars (used to 'row' through the air), seats, instruments and in short everything but the indispensable ballast were all discarded. Lunardi determined that the balloon was still too heavy so he climbed out, leaving his two passengers, Mr Biggins and Mrs Sage to take to the skies on their own. The press reported that both remained perfectly composed as the balloon first took a westerly direction

Captain Vincenzo Lunardi with his assistant George Biggin and Mrs Letitia Anne Sage, in a Balloon, John Francis Rigaud. (*Yale Center for British Art, Paul Mellon Collection*)

George Biggin, Julius Caesar Ibbetson. (*Yale Center for British Art, Paul Mellon Collection*)

before rising into another current and, crossing the Thames, headed north-west and remained in sight for quite some time. The pair were to travel as far as Harrow, where they made a safe landing in a rather angry farmer's field, from which they were rescued by some of the boys from Harrow School. There were rumours that the couple joined the 'mile high' club while embarking on this quest (Mrs Sage was seen on her knees in the basket of the balloon, but she claimed to have been lacing up an opening). Letitia recounted the story of her adventure in a letter to a friend which was published, but maybe she did not tell the whole story!

The 4th Earl (later 1st Marquess) of Cholmondeley made a bet at Brooks' – one of the many eccentric wagers placed in the notorious club – that he would ascend in a hot air balloon to a height of 6,000ft with his former mistress, the infamous courtesan Grace Dalrymple Elliott, by his side and 'perform in the aerial regions, the usual ceremonial rites, paid at the shrine of the laughter-loving queen'. The bet of 5,000 guineas was readily accepted by several men who thought the experiment impossible. Did this take place? We will never know.

George Biggin's Ascent in Lunardi's Balloon, Julius Caesar Ibbetson. (*Bayerische Staatsge-mäldesammlungen – Neue Pinakothek München*)

Grace Dalrymple Elliott,
Thomas Gainsborough.
(*Metropolitan Museum of Art*)

Chapter Seventeen

French Revolution: The Flight to Varennes

On the evening of 20 June 1791, Louis XVI and Marie Antoinette of France, together with their children and a handful of trusted attendants, made an ill-fated attempt to escape the revolutionary forces who were keeping them closely watched. The plan had taken many weeks to bring to fruition and the French queen, to whom it was inconceivable that she should survive without the everyday luxuries with which she was surrounded, had been engaged in smuggling various items to the safety of her sister in Brussels. An infamous Scottish courtesan played a key role in one of these transactions, risking her life in Marie Antoinette's service.

Grace Dalrymple Elliott, tall, willowy and stunningly beautiful, had gained her notoriety following a very public Criminal Conversation trial and divorce from her portly little husband, Dr (later Sir) John Eliot; Grace had been discovered in a Berkeley Row bagnio with her lover, the worthless Viscount Valentia who soon after discarded his mistress. The handsome Earl of Cholmondeley became her protector; tall and athletic, he was the perfect match for Grace, and the two made an attractive if slightly disreputable couple but, when a countess's coronet was not forthcoming, Grace left for France and the arms of Louis XVI's cousin, Louis Philippe Joseph, Duke d'Orléans (later known as Philippe Égalité). A brief interlude back in London followed where Grace bagged the affections of the young Prince of Wales and gained a permanent memento of her royal dalliance in the person of her daughter Georgiana, who the future monarch privately – if not publicly – acknowledged as his child. The Earl of Cholmondeley became the child's guardian and Grace, with an annuity from the royal purse, returned to her French duke, only to become trapped in Paris during the French Revolution.

During the summer of 1790 Grace took a house at Issy in the countryside surrounding the French capital, a fine if small Baroque château where d'Orléans often came to dine and which had been one of Marie Antoinette's favourite retreats. Anything that the château lacked in size was more than compensated for by the extensive gardens in which it stood. The queen and her family had been forcibly moved from Versailles to the Tuileries Palace where they were closely watched but Marie Antoinette was allowed, on two occasions, to walk in the gardens at Issy while Grace was living there. Grace – tactfully – kept her distance, allowing Marie Antoinette to stroll uninterrupted and lost in thought.

The situation for the royal family was dire. Aristocrats were fleeing France rather than stay and face the guillotine but Marie Antoinette had refused to leave without

Louis-Philippe de Bourbon, Duke of Orléans, after Sir Joshua Reynolds. (*Aberystwyth University School of Art Museum and Galleries*)

Queen Marie Antoinette of France and two of her Children Walking in The Park of Trianon, Adolf Ulrik Wertmüller. (*Nationalmuseum Sweden*)

the king, and Louis XVI prevaricated and obfuscated any schemes that were afoot. Finally, though, a plan was settled on. The royal children's governess, Louise-Élisabeth de Croÿ de Tourzel, the Marquise (later Duchess) de Tourzel would play the part of a Russian baroness (fictitiously named Madame de Korff) and the king and queen would disguise themselves as her servants, and together they would attempt to reach the royalist stronghold town of Montmédy just a short distance from the border with Belgium (then the Austrian Netherlands).

The French queen, assisted by her lady-in-waiting Madame Henriette Campan, began to move personal items ahead of the escape attempt. Completely ignoring the practicalities of the situation in which she found herself, the ever-regal Marie Antoinette needed a complete wardrobe for herself and the royal children at her destination. Madame Campan had to arrange for clothes and linen to be made up and sent, via a network of sympathizers, to the widow of the mayor of Arras who was one of the queen's women, ready to be taken from there to Brussels at a moment's notice. Other smaller items – deemed indispensable – were smuggled out of Paris by those loyal to the monarchy.

Grace had been in Brussels during the spring of 1790 while the Duke d'Orléans was on an extended visit to England. Belgium, like France, was in a state of turmoil with fighting between the Austrians and Brabant rebels who wanted independence, but the intrepid Mrs Elliott ventured there anyway and conducted business on behalf of the duke, speaking with his agents and banker. Why go to Brussels at a time when it was in a state of unrest? Why return to Paris when this too was fraught with danger and she could so easily have taken a boat to England? It has long been rumoured that Grace was involved in the murky world of espionage and she was certainly plucky enough. With her myriad of contacts both at home and on mainland Europe she could have passed messages and information on to those who needed them and it was not unknown for women, even of Grace's station in life, to operate in this way. What could have been more natural than that she should write to Lord Cholmondeley in England, who had the care of her young daughter, and that he should keep her informed of her child's progress? However, Cholmondeley had the ear of his close friend, the Prince of Wales, and so Grace may have knowingly been a conduit for undercover messages to be sent back and forth between the Duke d'Orléans and the prince. If so – whether she acted out of love, patriotism or for financial gain – Grace placed herself in a dangerous position.

Marie Antoinette's sister, the Archduchess Maria Christina, was resident in Brussels and, believing that Grace meant to return there, Marie Antoinette sent Madame Campan to Issy with a request that Grace should deliver a small box and a letter to the archduchess. Grace, even though a return trip had not been among her immediate plans, acquired a passport and duly made the journey, but arrived just after the archduchess had left. Instead, and in accordance with Marie Antoinette's instructions, she left the box and letter with General Johann Peter de Beaulieu at Mons, commander of the Austrian army, an act that suggests the beleaguered queen was, as she was later accused, plotting an alliance with the army of her homeland.

Louis XVI, King of France, Joseph Siffrède Duplessis (workshop of). (*Rijksmuseum*)

While Grace had played her part, the transportation of Marie Antoinette's dressing-case, her *nécessaire de toilette*, was a little more difficult for the queen and her attendants to arrange. This case held jars of ointment and perfumes and Marie Antoinette could not do without it. Being persuaded that if she sent it ostensibly as a gift to her sister in Brussels her intended escape would be revealed to all, Marie Antoinette instead arranged an elaborate plan whereby her sister's envoy asked publicly for her to arrange an identical one to be made and sent to the archduchess. However, by the time the escape was imminent, the dressing-case was still some six weeks from completion and in the hands of the ivory-turner. To leave her case behind was unthinkable for the queen and, in desperation, she announced, for the benefit of the guards and spies watching her, that as she had promised her sister the dressing-case, there was nothing to be done but empty her own and send it. It was Marie Antoinette's attachment to this indispensable item that partially uncovered her plan as the wardrobe woman knew she would never be parted from it and told the authorities of her suspicions. The escape attempt was ultimately doomed. Louis XVI and Marie Antoinette, their children and attendants fled from Paris on the evening of 20 June 1791 (the royal family disguised as servants to 'Madame de Korff' as planned), but were stopped at Varennes-en-Argonne. They arrived back in Paris a few days later as prisoners and under a heavy armed guard and Grace – probably wisely given her involvement in the plot – discreetly slipped out of the city on the same day and made for Spa in Belgium. It was claimed by Madame Campan that, overnight on the family's flight and capture, Marie Antoinette's hair 'turned white as that of a seventy-year-old woman'.

The ultimate fate of Louis XVI and Marie Antoinette is well-known: within three years of the escape attempt, which became known as the Flight to Varennes, they had both died on the guillotine, as did the Duke d'Orléans. Grace too faced further dangers: she eventually returned to Paris and bravely faced further predicaments including imprisonment, but managed to survive her ordeals.

George IV, when Prince of Wales, Sir William Beechey. (*Metropolitan Museum of Art*)

Chapter Eighteen

Brighton's Travelling Windmill

The breezy cliffs at Brighton in East Sussex were an ideal location for a windmill, and several had dotted the landscape for centuries.

By the late 1790s, the seaside town of Brighton, formerly known as Brighthelmstone, was enjoying a resurgence in its fortunes, due in large part to the Prince of Wales, later George IV, who helped turn it from a modest fishing village into a fashionable and fun resort when he began to visit. George first came to Brighton for his health as it was thought that sea-bathing would benefit him. He later lived in the town along with his 'wife', Maria Fitzherbert, a young and beautiful Catholic widow who the prince married in a secret morganatic ceremony unsanctioned by his father, the validity of which is still disputed to this day. Building work in the town was being carried on apace and Brighton was growing rapidly; the Prince of Wales enthusiastically transformed his house on the seafront into the Marine Pavilion and later, with the help of the architect John Nash, the extravagant Royal Pavilion we know today, and Mrs Fitzherbert discreetly had a private villa close by.

West Mill, a black post windmill, stood in open ground on the seafront, located on the edge of Belle Vue Fields (now Regency Square) and had been there since at least 1744. From 1792 both the mill and an associated bakery on West Street were operated by John Streeter, a well-known figure in Brighton who was held in high regard by the old townsfolk, if not by the influx of newcomers and visitors.

In 1793, a 10,000-strong military encampment was quartered for two months alongside the windmill, a response to the growing threat from France. This camp was used as a setting by Jane Austen in her novel *Pride and Prejudice* (Lydia Bennet spent time in Brighton where she delighted in the camp and her pursuit of the handsome but reprobate army officer George Wickham). In the years immediately after the soldiers had departed, the expanding town began to encroach onto Belle Vue Fields and the old mill became an eyesore and a nuisance to the well-heeled occupants of the newly-built town houses. They petitioned for it to be demolished.

However, Mr Streeter was not a man to bow to pressure and, rather than destroy his mill, he decided to move it – lock, stock and barrel – to a new location; an enormous undertaking but one which was not unheard of. A post mill is built

Perspective View of Brighthelmstone and of the Sea Coast as far as the Isle of Wight, A. Wallis after J. Lambert. (*Royal Pavilion & Museums, Brighton & Hove (CC BY-SA)*)

Bathing Machines at Brighton, Thomas Rowlandson. (*Royal Pavilion & Museums, Brighton & Hove (CC BY-SA)*)

Oxen Moving Mill, Percy Thomas Macquoid. (*Royal Pavilion & Museums, Brighton & Hove (CC BY-SA)*)

around a centre post – enabling it to be turned by winching the 'tail pole' so that the sails can catch the wind – and so, with jacks and levers, the whole structure could be lifted and moved. Neighbours and local 'gentleman farmers' all offered to help and, on 28 March 1797, fully intact other than its sails, West Mill was manoeuvred onto a contraption akin to skis and harnessed to a team of yoked oxen (accounts vary: contemporary newspaper reports say thirty-six oxen, later accounts eighty-six, and the painting of the event certainly shows more than thirty-six beasts).

A huge concourse of people gathered at dawn to watch with bated breath as the mill made its momentous journey westward across fields and country lanes to its new home on the Dyke Road near the village of Preston (now merged with the urban sprawl of Brighton and Hove), just over a mile away. Once safely relocated,

Near Regents Square, Brighton, W. Daniell. (*Royal Pavilion & Museums, Brighton & Hove (CC BY-SA)*)

John Streeter carried on his business as usual, the only difference being his mill's name. It subsequently went through a variety – Streeter's, Black, Dyke, Preston and finally Trusler's Mill – before it was eventually pulled down in the 1880s almost a century after it had first been threatened with demolition.

You might have thought that one public exploit might have been enough for 'honest' John Streeter (as he was known), but no, two decades later he was to be found entertaining a crowd once more. After visiting Lindfield Fair he accepted an old friend's invitation to stay the night and, after what would seem to have been a boozy evening with a few tales told, Mr Streeter was reminded of working as a ploughboy for his host, Henry Steven's father. Mr Stevens senior was still hale and hearty at 90 years of age and on the next day, to the delight of a number of spectators who had gathered to watch, he officiated as ploughboy to John Streeter, the old man shouting 'gee ho, Dobbin' as they drove off. Their task completed, Henry Stevens, 60 years old, took the reins followed by his son and then his 5-year-old grandson. After this inter-generational ploughing exhibition, a wholesome and very welcome ploughman's dinner was served to one and all.

Margaret Nicholson, Attempting to Assassinate His Majesty, George III, at the Garden Entrance of St James's Palace, 2 August 1786, Robert Dighton. (*Yale Center for British Art, Paul Mellon Collection*)

Chapter Nineteen

To Kill the King: Frith the Madman

Assassination attempts upon monarchs have happened throughout history and there were several attempts made upon the life of King George III. The first was made by a woman in June 1777: Hannah Banks, of very genteel appearance, was charged with attempting to assault the king as he was travelling from St James's to the Theatre Royal by breaking the side glass of his chair and behaving in an outrageous manner. As she appeared to be in a state of insanity, the court delivered her into the care of her friends who promised to take care of her.

The next attempt was also made by a woman. In 1786 Margaret Nicholson tried to stab the king using an ivory-handled dessert knife as he was alighting from his coach. Deemed insane, Margaret was committed to Bethlem Hospital for the remainder of her life (she died on 14 May 1828). Medical reviews of her condition while in Bethlem confirmed her continued insanity and, by the end of her life, she was also totally deaf.

A theme of insanity is evident in these crimes, and it was no different in the case of John Frith, the third of the would-be assassins. On 21 January 1790, Frith, dressed in scarlet with an orange cockade, threw a stone at the king's coach as it travelled to the State Opening of Parliament. He was immediately arrested and charged with treason.

John was born on 15 March 1752 in St James's, Westminster, the younger son (he had an older brother named James) of John Frith senior, a distiller of Glasshouse Street, St James (a man who had formerly served with distinction in the Life Guards). His mother, Esther, née Davis, died young and was buried at St John's parish church, Hampstead and John senior died in 1769, leaving his two sons to the care of friends. John lived, for a time, with Edward Blackshaw, a Covent Garden haberdasher.

James travelled east to India as a lieutenant with the EIC but almost immediately fell ill while in camp at Tiruchirappalli in Tamil Nadu and died there on 16 November 1771, aged just 21. Everything he had he left to his younger brother.

Left almost alone in the world, Frith, it was later said, 'indulged too freely in the dissipated pleasures of the town, and soon spent the scanty fruits of parental industry'. A family friend, David Burnsall, an auctioneer from Chelsea, went so far as to bar young John from his home. Running out of options and using the money left to him by his brother, in 1774 Frith purchased a commission as an ensign in

Bethlem Hospital (at Moorfields), unknown artist. (*Wellcome Collection*)

the 37th Regiment of Foot. Initially army life must have suited him and he was promoted to lieutenant within the regiment a year later, but he retired in 1778.

Four years later, and with the help of Mr Burnsall, John Frith exchanged into the 10th (North Lincolnshire) Regiment of Foot. During his service with the 10th Regiment he was posted to the West Indies and it was there that his madness began to manifest itself; in 1786 he was asked to leave the regiment and placed on half-pay, to his extreme resentment. For the next twenty years, John Frith remained on the army lists as a half-pay officer on the books of the 2nd Battalion of the 1st Regiment of Foot.

Prior to the attempt on the king's life, John was clearly unwell and grieving the loss of his family; he arranged for a memorial for them at the parish church where his mother was buried:

George III, Sir William Beechey.
(*National Library of Australia*)

Upon his tomb is this singular inscription, under an emblematical device representing a rainbow, beneath which is the sun within a double triangle: 'And there shall be a standard of Truth erected in the west, which shall overpower the enemy.'——May 12, 1786, 'This glorious phænomena in Sol of the Almighty came down for my protection in latitude 15, on the Bahama sandbanks, and where the spiritual cities of Sodom and Gomorrah came up in the West Indies. Vide Revelations. Your dying embers shall again revive, the phænix souls of Friths are still alive.'

Frith disappeared until, on 29 December 1789, he publicly read from a document he had written, *A Protest Against the Democracy of the People of the Kingdom of Great Britain*, in which he referred to witchcraft and people's mental faculties being endangered. A few weeks later, on 21 January 1790 and as the king rode in his carriage along to the House of Lords, Frith picked up the largest stone he could find and threw it at the king. The stone landed harmlessly against the carriage window and the king barely noticed, but Frith was immediately arrested. Upon

His Majesty King George III returning to Town from Windsor with an Escort of 10th Prince of Wales' Own Light Dragoons, Charles Turner after Richard Barrett Davis. (*Yale Center for British Art, Paul Mellon Collection*)

FRITH the MAD MAN *HURLING* TREASON *at the* KING.

Frith the Madman Hurling Treason at the King, Isaac Cruikshank. (*Yale Center for British Art, Paul Mellon Collection*)

being questioned, he claimed that his only regret was that the stone had missed its target but that his intention had only been to attract the king's attention.

During his interrogation, it became clear to all that he was in a 'state of deranged mind'. A bag found upon him contained a copy of what he called his 'Manifesto'; the original of this document was the one he had stuck on the wall of the courtyard in St James's some three weeks previously. It contained a jumble of incoherencies, confirmation of his 'derangement', and he was sent to Newgate prison to await his trial for treason but was judged mentally unfit to plead. Instead, Frith was transferred to Bethlem from where, on 17 December 1791, he was released to his friends and disappeared from view except for his inclusion in the army lists as a half-pay officer up to and including the 1806 list after which, presumably, his death occurred.

James Hadfield, aged 44 and a former soldier, made the last attempt on the king's life. On 15 May 1800, at the Theatre Royal, Drury Lane, he fired a pistol at the king who was standing in the royal box during the playing of the national anthem. Hadfield missed but was charged with high treason and – like the others before him – was pronounced insane and admitted to Bethlem Hospital, where he remained until his death in 1842. The king was unharmed and his calm reaction was much praised and widely reported, so much so that a medal was struck by Matthew Boulton's Soho Mint in Birmingham to mark the event.

Despite these attempts upon his life, George III lived until 1820.

Chapter Twenty

The Norwich Nymph: A Female Jockey

For eight years, Alicia Massingham lived with the flamboyant but eccentric 'Sporting' Colonel Thomas Thornton as his wife, by his side when he toured France in 1802 following the Peace of Amiens and presiding as mistress of his Yorkshire mansion, Thornville Royal (now known as Allerton Castle) near Knaresborough in North Yorkshire. Alicia was a beauty, with blonde curls and a fine figure, but she had another attribute which endeared her just as much as her appearance to the colonel; she was the most accomplished horsewoman of her era.

Born on 22 August 1781 at Fakenham in Norfolk, Alice (as she was christened) was the youngest daughter of John Massingham, a clock-maker, but she wanted more than a quiet life in rural Norfolk. By her teens Alice had travelled to the capital, altered her name to the more fashionable Alicia and found employment as an equestrian performer at Astley's Amphitheatre in Lambeth, a hugely popular circus.

Her beauty and courage attracted a score of admirers and soon Alicia left Lambeth and Astley's in the company of her wealthy lover, the sporting colonel. Thornton, who was around thirty years older than Alicia, had everything good fortune could bestow bar a title. He was wealthy, well-educated and of good family, had served as lieutenant colonel with the West Yorkshire Militia (until leaving in 1795 after a disagreement), and entertained the Prince of Wales at his Yorkshire estate. He was renowned as a *bon vivant* and the leading sportsman of his day. His stable was well-stocked with thoroughbreds, he hunted with guns, hounds and falcons just about anything that moved, was an accomplished angler and excelled at athletics. In 1802, following the Peace of Amiens and the cessation of war with France, the colonel crossed the Channel for a 'sporting tour' with an enormous entourage, an artist, valet, gamekeeper and huntsman: he contrived to meet Napoléon Bonaparte and present him with a gold-inlaid three-barrelled flintlock pistol believed to be the only gun given by an Englishman to the future French emperor. In a specially-built carriage, designed with compartments housing not only his guns, fishing rods and other sporting paraphernalia but also his fox-hounds, Thornton travelled in comfort with his 'wife' beside him. To the world at large, Alicia passed as Mrs Thornton but much as she held out hope of achieving that position, a betrothal had not been forthcoming.

Astley's Amphitheatre. (*Microcosm of London (1808–1810)*)

Thornville Royal was the scene for many a sporting party and, in the summer of 1804, Captain Flint was staying there with his own mistress, a woman named Amelia. Popular gossip claimed that Alicia and Amelia were sisters, but they were only related in that they were both of the sisterhood of the female *coterie*. Alicia was the centre of attention; her astounding horsemanship won her admirers by the dozen and led to a wager. A race was to be run, at the Knavesmire racecourse in York, between Alicia and her 'brother-in-law', Captain Flint, using two of the colonel's best horses: both Thornton and Alicia bet heavily on the outcome, expecting that she would win. Alicia wagered 500 guineas on herself and Thornton double that sum, but Flint was no gentleman and he subtly rigged proceedings in his favour.

Emperor Napoleon I,
François-Pascal Simon
baron Gérard (workshop of).
(*Rijksmuseum*)

At four o'clock on race day, Alicia appeared seated on Vingarillo and led by her colonel; Flint was not far behind on Thornville and the race started minutes later. It was estimated that the crowd at the Knavesmire was 100,000 at least, and a company of the 6th Light Dragoons were on hand to keep the course clear. There had been rumours that Alicia would ride 'man-style' in breeches but on the day – to the crowd's disappointment – she rode side-saddle in a dress that had a leopard-coloured bodice, blue sleeves and a buff skirt, a blue cap hiding her curls. Captain Flint was all in white.

Before they began, Flint ordered Alicia peremptorily to his left, shouting at her to 'Keep that side, Ma'am!' which meant that she was unable to use her whip. Despite this, and even though her horse was smaller, the skilful Alicia took the lead for the first 3 miles but then fell behind in the last when her horse became lame.

A View of the Race between Mrs Thornton and Mr Flint of York. (*York Museums Trust – http:// yorkmuseumstrust.org.uk – Public Domain*)

She thought Flint would pull up and declare the race null and void but loath to lose the bet, he galloped over the finishing line. Alicia, stung by his callousness, called him out publicly in the papers and challenged him to a re-match the following year. Thornton refused to pay up on a wager made with Flint, saying it had merely been a 'show bet' to increase interest. With resentment simmering on all sides, the matter was left unresolved for the time being.

The race, however, turned Alicia into an overnight celebrity and she was invited back to Astley's to view their latest entertainment featuring songs, dances and action, *York Races, or the Female Jockey*. She was only 23 and fame turned her head. Everyone lauded the skill of 'the Nymph of Norwich' but, for all she was

York City during the Races, Thomas Rowlandson. (*York Museums Trust – http://yorkmuseumstrust. org.uk – Public Domain*)

thinly-veiled for the sake of respectability as the colonel's wife, she was nothing more than a good-time girl living for the moment, her future security dependent upon Thornton's whims. Thornton, a sportsman to the core, was no stranger to a sporting wager and entertained lavishly, his fortune liable to fluctuate alarmingly. By the end of the year, Thornville Royal was sold to clear his debts and ensure an income. Christmas 1804, the last before he had to surrender the mansion to its new owner, was one long month of celebrations, field-sports during the day and carousing with his guests in the evenings. The colonel then took a fine furnished house known as The Boudoir on the Westminster Bridge Road in Lambeth. (In a twist of fate, Thornville Royal was transferred back to him two years later.)

The re-match took place in August 1805, again at the Knavesmire but although Flint attended, he declined to race. A Mr Bomfield was to match himself against Alicia, but at the last minute he pulled out and so the lady contented herself with cantering in style around the course for the crowd's entertainment. Afterwards, she raced the most celebrated jockey of the day, Frank Buckle of Newmarket. Alicia was dressed in a purple cap and waistcoat, a nankeen skirt and purple shoes with embroidered stockings, Buckle in a blue cap and jacket with white sleeves, and the two riders were evenly matched although, in fairness, Alicia had a weight advantage which proved key. She took an early lead, only to lose it to Buckle and then gain it back, winning by half a neck.

Captain Flint, meanwhile, sought out Colonel Thornton among a crowd of ladies and took a horsewhip to his shoulders in retribution for their dispute over the previous wager. The colonel, ever litigious (Alicia would later dub him Old Bailey Thornton), took his revenge in the courtroom.

Then, with the colonel's finances in further disarray, Alicia's days as 'Mrs Thornton' came to an end:

PROVINCIAL MISCELLANIES

Elopement extraordinary! – A few days ago eloped, with a bold son of Mars, the celebrated equestrian Lady, Mrs Alicia Thornton, *cara sposa* of the equally celebrated Colonel Thornton! – As soon as the dire intelligence reached the Boudoir, the myrtles in the bow-window lost their lovely verdure – the rose-buds of Venus languished, drooped and died – even the old greyhound hung his head, and seemed to mourn the loss of departed beauty. Not so the enraged Colonel. He had just finished his second bottle, and, starting up with pot-valiant impetuosity, swore he would inflict certain death upon all the parties concerned in the *enlevement* of his faithless fair; but instantly recollecting that she had run away with a jockey of martial blood and mettle, he paused, sat down, called for another bottle, and consoled himself with the prospect of much completer revenge, by bringing an action of damages against the young hero.

It wasn't long before answers to the above appeared in the newspapers. Far from being a 'son of Mars', the gentleman in question was really an 'old son of Neptune', Lieutenant Harries, RN, well past the first flush of youth and with the added encumbrances of both a wife and a mistress, the latter (possibly Amelia) hastily discarded in favour of Alicia:

> Alas! poor deluded ALICIA, when thou hast parted with the Colonel's last present (your new pelisse), to supply the exigencies of the moment, then will this boastful Son of MARS retreat to the empire of *Neptune*, and securing his own sweet person, abandon you (as he has done Mrs F.), to your sorrowful fate.

Sadly for Alicia, this warning was to prove all too prophetic. She was two months pregnant when she decamped and the colonel had been aware of this fact (it is not known if the child she was carrying – a boy – was the colonel's or the lieutenant's). Perhaps Alicia had chanced one more roll of the dice in the hope that a pregnancy would induce the colonel to make her his lawful wife? If so, she failed. Alicia had everything the colonel could desire in a woman apart from a fortune, and a wealthy wife was what the colonel now needed. Just weeks later, at St Mary's in Lambeth, he married an heiress, Eliza Cawston of Mundon Hall in Essex. A year later Eliza gave birth to a son, William Thomas Thornton.

Neither Eliza's fortune nor the marriage lasted long and by 1815 Thornton had all but sold up in England and relocated to France where he rented the Château de Chambord, a former royal residence near Blois which had been abandoned during the French Revolution and was semi-derelict (he lived largely in the outbuildings). With delusions of grandeur, the colonel styled himself Marquis de Pont and Prince de Chambord, bought the estate of Pont le Roi at St Aube and applied to become a naturalized Frenchman. Thornton might have been on a downward spiral, but Alicia had already hit rock bottom. Her son, George, had been born in November 1809 in a house on South Molton Street and Alicia went on to have two further children, a daughter named Georgina Alice and a son, Ernest, who was born inside the Fleet Prison while Alicia was imprisoned for debt, both their fathers unknown. By 1817 she was living in the Westminster area but claiming poor relief for herself and her children.

Colonel Thornton had a new mistress, a Devonian woman from a dissenting family, named Priscilla Duins by whom he had two daughters. The extravagantly-named Thornvillia Diana Rockingham Thornton (so-called for his long-lost Yorkshire estate, and his favourite hunter!), was born in November 1816, christened in Paris the following May and then in St Mary St Marylebone two years later; the colonel was formulating a plan to acknowledge this illegitimate daughter as his heir. His will, written in 1818, left just £100 to his son (who was enrolled in a

French college), nothing at all to his abandoned wife and everything else in trust for his daughter and for the benefit of Priscilla. For reasons that are unclear, he did not alter this will when his second daughter, Maria St Hubert Thornton, was born in 1820. After Thornton's death in 1823, his wife mounted a legal challenge on behalf of her son to have the will declared null and void. Ultimately though, Priscilla had a more practical solution to the predicament. To secure her daughters' inheritance, three years after the sporting colonel's death she simply kept things in the family and married his 19-year-old son.

Fleet Prison. (*Microcosm of London* (*1808–1810*))

Chapter Twenty-One

Martha Udny, aka 'Mrs Nibs'

Martha Udny was one of the two sub-governesses to Princess Charlotte of Wales, the only (legitimate) daughter and heir of the Prince of Wales. Charlotte famously hated Mrs Udny, labelling her 'Mrs Nibs'; gossipy and bosomy, Martha was a handsome-looking woman but fond of a drink and – reputedly – also of men. The princess and the royal household were perhaps in ignorance of Mrs Udny's background. The woman who was tutoring the heir to the throne was actually the daughter of a Presbyterian brewer from Leman Street in Whitechapel, an area now more renowned for the murders that were committed by 'Jack the Ripper' in the late nineteenth-century.

Martha was baptized on 24 January 1757, the eldest child and only daughter of Thomas Jordan and his wife, also named Martha. The family were 'trade', members of the burgeoning middle classes. When she was 30 years of age, Martha made a spectacularly good marriage to Robert Fullarton Udny, a widower much older than she, who owned a fine house in Teddington and also his hereditary estate of Udny Castle in Aberdeenshire (although the latter was in a state of disrepair). Robert Udny, according to the Prince of Wales (who was as much of a gossip as Mrs Udny!), was hideously ugly but incredibly wealthy due to his career as a West Indian merchant. With his vast fortune, Robert indulged in his great passion: art. Udny's collection of masterpieces was widely admired and the miniaturist Richard Cosway was one of Robert's closest friends.

Robert Udny died in 1802 and his widow was subsequently offered her position within the royal household, to the dismay of Princess Charlotte who variously described her new sub-governess as cross, a great goose, selfish, bad-tempered and a drunk. When she was 10 years old, the princess made her 'will', a childish document but one which showed her affection, or lack of it, for the people around her. Dr Nott, Lady de Clifford and Mrs Campbell (Charlotte's chaplain, governess and sub-governess respectively) were clearly well thought of by their young charge, but not so 'Mrs Nibs'. Charlotte wrote, 'nothing to Mrs. Udney, for reasons'.

Lady de Clifford and Dr Nott believed that Mrs Udny had shown the young princess a rude cartoon which lampooned Nelson's mistress, Lady Hamilton, and

Opposite: Mrs Martha Udny, John Massey Wright after Richard Cosway. (*Yale Center for British Art, Paul Mellon Fund*)

Carlton House, North Front, Richard Gilson Reeve after William Westall. (*Yale Center for British Art, Paul Mellon Collection*)

had then made bad worse by explaining the meaning of it to the child. They saw a chance to have Mrs Udny disciplined and perhaps even dismissed, but Martha got wind of their plan and struck first. Princess Charlotte had her own royal household in Montague House, a mansion that stood adjacent to the Prince of Wales's grand London home, Carlton House, so he could keep an eye on his daughter. Martha went to the prince and whispered in his ear that Dr Nott was gossiping with the young princess, encouraging her to be disrespectful to her royal father and, in the end, it was Nott who lost his position.

There were rumours of lovers: Lady Harcourt suggested that Mrs Udny had indulged in an intrigue with an unnamed tutor belonging to the royal household. The Duke of Cumberland (the Prince of Wales's younger brother and future King of Hanover) flirted with and teased the sub-governess, and even waltzed with her at a ball. Charlotte cattily described it as 'a *most amusing* scene as you can *well conceive*.' Martha was even reputed to have had an affair with Cosway after her husband's death.

Lady Hamilton with a dog, unknown artist after George Romney. (*Yale Center for British Art, Paul Mellon Collection*)

Princess Charlotte of Wales, George Dawe. (*Museum of New Zealand, Te Papa Tongarewa*)

In 1813, Mrs Udny and Lady de Clifford both resigned from their positions. At her death, on 1 September 1831, Martha bequeathed several items relating to Charlotte which she had kept over the years, a bible in two volumes and a prayer book which had been given to her by the princess, a miniature depicting the princess with a dog and a bust of Charlotte. Perhaps, after all, Mrs Martha Udny was not the louche person Charlotte imagined her to be but simply a woman from a humble background who struggled to fit in; a lady whose life – via a good marriage – led her from Whitechapel to Windsor Castle and the charge of the heir to the throne.

NB: Martha's surname is invariably spelt as Udney: Martha and her husband used Udny, as have we.

Chapter Twenty-Two

King of the Resurrection Men

When we think of body-snatching, the names that instantly come to mind are the notorious duo Burke and Hare, but they were not the only people involved in this dark practice. William Millard was named as the 'King of the Resurrection Men' by the public newspapers, but was he deserving of that title?

William Millard was born in the early 1780s and married his second wife Ann Hunter in August 1808, at St Botolph-without-Bishopgate church in the City of London. The couple had six children between 1809 and 1822, during which time William was employed at St Thomas's hospital, then located in Southwark. Originally an anatomist, by 1814 William had risen to the position of superintendent of the anatomy theatre which was headed by the leading surgeon, Sir Astley Paston Cooper.

During the winter of 1821 William became ill and although he didn't take up the offer, Sir Astley Cooper offered him the use of his holiday home for his recuperation. William's health continued to deteriorate until, in 1822, he was made redundant, with testimonials of good conduct. At the suggestion of medical students from the hospital, William set up a hostelry, but this was to be a short-lived venture as he had little business acumen and lost money. He approached Sir Astley to seek help but was advised that it would take some time to secure him employment elsewhere.

In July 1823, the family's lives were turned upside-down when William was arrested together with an accomplice, Cornelius Fitzgerald. The pair were charged with being found 'in possession of the body of a female'. The local constable had met the prisoners in the Great Maze Pond, Southwark, at half past five in the morning, carrying a box on their shoulders. Naturally suspicious, the officer called to them asking what they were doing. Cornelius immediately fled the scene, leaving William to carry the can, or in this case the corpse. The corpse was taken to St Olave's workhouse, Cornelius was soon apprehended and the pair were granted bail to appear later at court.

They duly appeared before the court and were sentenced to three months' hard labour in the Coldbath Fields prison, informally known as 'The Steel'. While admitting he had taken the body, William claimed that the hospital was fully aware of what he was doing; he expected to be found not guilty and be released.

St Botolphs, John Chapman after unknown artist.
(*Yale Center for British Art, Paul Mellon Collection*)

William appealed but was unsuccessful. His worried wife, Ann, tried in vain to visit her husband, even sneaking letters in with his linen to try to ascertain his health, but she could do little to help when William was taken seriously ill. Ann visited him in the prison's infirmary before his death. The following report is from the coroner's inquest:

> T.W Unwin, Esq, Coroner, on the body of William Millard, aged 43, a notorious resurrectionist confined in the prison. Mr. Christmas, clerk to the prison, said, that the deceased was sentenced at the last Middlesex Sessions to six months imprisonment. John Smith, a prisoner, stated that he attended the deceased as nurse; he was unwell, and on the 27th of September was removed to the infirmary, by order of Mr. Webb, the surgeon; he complained of a slight cold, and Mr. Webb ordered some medicines, which the witness administered to him; he was also regularly attended by Mr. Webb, and was also visited by four or five physicians; he had such a diet as was suitable to his condition. Four days later William's condition deteriorated until he died at half past nine on the morning of October 14th, 1823.

However, this was not the end of the story. Ann was now a widow with six young mouths to feed and she began a battle to clear her husband's name, placing the blame for his death squarely at the feet of the medical profession who she thought should have done more to help him. More darkly, she hinted that there was a conspiracy taking place. Around two years after William's death, Ann wrote and published a pamphlet, *An Account of the Circumstances Attending the Imprisonment and Death of the Late William Millard*. In this, she made claims about how bodies were procured for dissection in the London hospitals and gave examples of bad practice. While it was illegal to steal a corpse from a public graveyard to sell to the dissecting theatres, the rules were bent by unscrupulous men in the employment of the hospitals. Graves in the hospital grounds, where those with no friends to claim their bodies were buried, were routinely plundered to supply the anatomical students at the hospitals with subjects upon which to practise.

It was claimed that one of St Thomas's porters frequently targeted any friendless person who applied for admission to the hospital, charitably offering to be the security for the expense of their burial if they died within the hospital's precincts. If the patient recovered, the porter had lost nothing but if they died he then reneged on his bargain and sold their body to the dissecting room for a fee of 4 guineas. The Borough Gang, under the protection of Sir Astley Paston Cooper, were notorious grave-robbers. In 1816 they tried to get the price of a corpse raised from 4 to

Opposite: Water Engine, Cold-Bath-Fields Prison. (*Microcosm of London (1808–1810)*)

St Thomas's Hospital, London, unknown artist. (*Wellcome Collection*)

6 guineas and, when thwarted, refused to supply cadavers to the dissecting room at St Thomas's Hospital for some months. William Millard, however, had used his myriad of contacts to lawfully keep the students in his anatomy theatre supplied with fresh corpses, to the fury of the gang but the gratitude of Sir Astley. Little wonder then, with these dark secrets in his past, that William had believed his former patron would help him in his predicament.

Ann, in her pamphlet, gave a different account of her husband's activities on the night in question. William had, she claimed, been invited to the graveyard of the London Hospital (now the Royal London Hospital) on Whitechapel Road by Mr Hurst, the surgeon's beadle, to claim a recently-deceased patient from a newly-dug grave in the hospital grounds. The London Hospital's anatomical school was permanently supplied by the bodies of those who had all too recently been patients in the establishment and not claimed by relatives but instead – temporarily – buried in the grounds of the hospital. In the heat of the summer months, the

A sky-lit anatomy theatre with anatomical specimens in jars and a suspended skeleton, J.C. Stadler after A. Pugin. (*Wellcome Collection*)

hospital sometimes had more corpses than they could practicably deal with and so offered them for sale to their fellow anatomists. It was an informal arrangement between the various London hospitals that occurred on a regular basis. Rather than send an agent to collect the body offered to him, on that fateful August night in 1823, William went himself. No sooner had he entered the grounds attached to the London Hospital than he was set upon by a number of patients and police officers, alerted by Hurst's rival in the trade in bodies at the London Hospital, Samuel Hicks (also known as Sam the Barber) who was a hospital porter and also shaved the patients. As William had not had the chance to commit any offence, he had been charged under the Vagrant Act and sent to prison.

Ann's endeavours ultimately came to nothing, despite shining a very bright light onto the trade in bodies between the hospitals which, while endorsed by several distinguished surgeons, raised the question of whether it was morally if not legally wrong. She failed to improve her situation; in fact, all she succeeded in doing was to alienate the few acquaintances she still had in the London hospitals and medical schools.

So, was William Millard the King of the Resurrection Men, or simply a trustworthy employee of the medical profession carrying out a vital role and furthering the anatomical knowledge of the students by supplying them with bodies upon which they could practise and learn? We'll leave that decision up to you.

Chapter Twenty-Three

Caroline Crachami: The Sicilian Fairy

Lewis Foghil was born around 1792 in Palermo, Sicily. At the age of 17, he joined the *Chasseurs Britanniques*, a military regiment formed during the French Revolution and initially comprising French *émigrés* who fought for the British. When the regiment became part of Wellington's army during the Peninsular War, Lewis saw action at Salamanca for which he received the Peninsular Medal. Whilst in Ireland during July 1814, Lewis was discharged from the *Chasseurs* and, almost straight away, at Mallow in Cork, enlisted in the 40th Regiment of Foot, the 'Fighting Fortieth', as a trumpeter. Just before enlisting, however, he met and married a young Irish girl, Margaret Norton.

The 40th was sent to New Orleans as part of the British force fighting the war of 1812, and Margaret followed the army in the baggage train. She had probably just realized that she was pregnant and, not knowing how long her new husband would be overseas, took the decision to travel with him, despite whatever dangers lay ahead. It was later claimed (by the surgeon, Sir Everard Home) that during a storm in the middle of the night, a monkey had found its way inside a tent and had bitten Margaret's finger, an event that was believed to have had far-reaching consequences.

After a short time in the US, the 40th was ordered to Flanders in support of Wellington's troops and so, on 18 June 1815, the Foghils found themselves at the Battle of Waterloo.

The 1st Battalion of the 40th Foot, commanded by Captain James Lowrey and part of Lambert's Brigade, defended the farmhouse at La Haye Sainte, a pivotal area of the battle. The British and German troops were completely outnumbered by the French but held out amid fierce fighting until late afternoon. Had Napoléon's army captured La Haye Sainte earlier in the day, the outcome of the battle would have been very different. For his part in this battle, Lewis received the Waterloo medal.

So, you might well ask, what does all this military history have to do with Caroline, the 'Sicilian Fairy'? The answer is that Lewis Foghil was her father and she was – reputedly – born amid the chaos on the day after the Battle of Waterloo and with a form of dwarfism: she was a primordial dwarf and reportedly only 7in tall and weighing just one pound when born. The bite from the monkey was suggested as the cause for Caroline's diminutive stature, such were the beliefs at that time.

The Battle of Waterloo, Jan Willem Pieneman. (*Rijksmuseum*)

Margaret Foghil continued to travel with her husband, giving birth to a healthy son, Charles, at Ribécourt-Dreslincourt in northern France before the family returned to Ireland and, in 1821, Lewis was discharged from the army. He had a pulmonary affliction and had suffered a sabre wound during action. Immediately, Lewis joined the Royal Lancers but a year later he left, having 'not answered the purpose for which he enlisted'.

Lewis, a trumpeter, turned to his musical abilities and possibly through Margaret's connections (she was the sister of an actor named Mr King), he found employment in the orchestra at the Theatre Royal in Dublin. More children followed, none of whom suffered from the dwarfism that afflicted Caroline.

What of Caroline? By the age of 9, she had only reached the height of 20in and was the size of a doll, weighing a mere 5 pounds and speaking in a strange, shrill voice. She was described as 'an extraordinary phenomenon'.

Caroline's walk was tottering and – magpie-like – she was entranced by anything shiny or glittery and liked fine clothes. Having been examined, poked and prodded

The Show, print by Rowney & Forster after John Augustus Atkinson. (*Yale Center for British Art, Paul Mellon Collection*)

by doctors all her short life, Caroline had an intense dislike of the medical profession and would shake her tiny fist at them to show her displeasure. Her speech was imperfect and this, combined with her assumed surname of Crachami, allowed Caroline to be passed off as Sicilian by birth.

Caroline's gullible parents were persuaded by Gilligan, a doctor who was treating her for a cough, that the air in Dublin was not conducive to her health and that she should go to London where the climate was better. He offered to do this at his own expense, but on the basis that her parents permitted her to be exhibited.

On reaching London, the 'Sicilian Fairy' became an exhibit at 22 New Bond Street where, for 2 shillings and 6 pence, you could view and touch the child: upwards of 200 people a day crowded into the rooms. Caroline became merely a commodity to provide entertainment for those who were obsessed with the rare and unusual and who would pay handsomely in pursuit of seeing these wonders. Proving an instant hit with the public and the nobility, Caroline was even presented to King George IV at Carlton House.

However, all was not well. Caroline's health, far from improving, took a turn for the worse: she was exhausted, suffering from tuberculosis and died on Friday, 4 June 1824 according to the Donation Book at the Royal College of Surgeons. This was not, however, the end of her story.

Her parents learned of their daughter's death from the newspapers and immediately set off for London to arrange for her burial. Arriving at Gilligan's lodgings, they were informed that he had left, taking Caroline's body with him. All that remained was her tiny bed and clothing. Frantic with worry, Lewis went to Sir Everard Home's house and was greeted by him on the misapprehension that

Royal College of Surgeons, Lincoln's Inn Fields, London, unknown artist. (*Wellcome Collection*)

The Royal College of Surgeons, Lincoln's Inn Fields, London: the interior of the Hunterian Museum, E. Radclyffe after Thomas Hosmer Shepherd. (*Wellcome Collection*)

he had been sent by Gilligan for the money: Gilligan and Home had, between them, submitted Caroline's body to the College of Surgeons for dissection. Some members of the college had previously offered Gilligan £500 for Caroline's remains, should anything untoward happen to her.

Lewis set off to reclaim his daughter's body but, on arriving at the college, he was devastated to find that the dissection had already taken place. He had no choice but to leave her there and to return with his wife to his family in Ireland. No burial took place and her body remains at the Hunterian Museum as an exhibit to this day. Dr Gilligan was assumed to have fled to France with the £1,500 he made from exhibiting poor little Caroline.

After Caroline's death, Lewis re-joined the army as a band master with the 60th Foot, the King's Own Rifle Brigade, continuing in that regiment until 1842 and ending his days in Perth playing in the house band of the Marquis of Breadalbane, a private brass band at Taymouth Castle, near Kenmore in the Highlands of Scotland.

Chapter Twenty-Four

The Dramatic Life of Jonathan Martin, tanner

I n a small cell, inside York Castle's prison, a stout middle-aged man of average height and with large red bushy whiskers sat for his portrait. Jonathan Martin had become something of a *cause célèbre*, gaining notoriety when he attempted to raze York Minster Cathedral to the ground.

Jonathan was born 43 years earlier, at Highside House near Hexham in Northumberland. His father, William Fenwick Martin, followed the eclectic and somewhat itinerant trades of soldier, tanner and fencing-master, and his growing brood of children was often left in the care of maternal relatives, particularly Jonathan's strict Methodist grandmother. Jonathan had a troubled childhood: 'tongue-tied' until he was 6 and cured by an operation, four years later he witnessed the death of his younger sister and playmate, Isabel. He recalled that the young girl was pushed down a set of stone steps by a neighbour, Peggy Hobuck, an act of cruelty from which Isabel died.

Apprenticed to a tanner, Jonathan decided that he wanted more from life and moved to London in search of travelling to 'foreign countries'. He achieved his aim, but not quite how he planned: Jonathan was press-ganged into the navy. For six years, Jonathan sailed the seas at a time when Britain was at war and saw action several times, notably in the Second Battle of Copenhagen in 1807 where the British fleet bombarded the Danish capital. Perhaps it was no wonder, after everything he had undergone, that he began to have visions, manifested in prophetic and vivid dreams.

After leaving the navy, Jonathan returned to the north-east and his profession of tanner. In the late summer of 1812, at the village of Norton, Durham, he married Martha Carter, a woman around fifteen years his senior and just over a year later their only child was born, a son named Richard for one of Jonathan's brothers. (Richard senior was a quartermaster in the British army and served in the Peninsular War and at the Battle of Waterloo.) The deaths of both of Jonathan's parents around this time further disrupted his mind and wellbeing: Jonathan embraced Methodism, becoming a Wesleyan preacher vehemently opposed to the Church of England – sometimes violently – and his mania culminated in him threatening to shoot the Bishop of Oxford. For this, Jonathan was arrested, declared insane and held in lunatic asylums at West Auckland and Gateshead, escaping from the latter in 1820 but only for three days before being recaptured.

York Minster, West Front of the Cathedral Church, Charles Wild. (*York Museums Trust – http://
yorkmuseumstrust.org.uk – Public Domain*)

Jonathan Martin, Edward Lin(d)ley. (*York Museums Trust – http://yorkmuseumstrust.org.uk – Public Domain*)

Martha stayed loyal to her husband and moved to Gateshead, near Newcastle, to be near his asylum. Possibly unknown to Jonathan, Martha was dying from breast cancer. Afterwards, when it was discovered that most of her household possessions were missing, Jonathan believed they had been stolen by the authorities, for the rest of his life calling it 'an old debt' and claiming he was owed around £24. In fact, Martha had sold them to buy opium to relieve her pain. She was buried in Gateshead in 1821 aged 52, and Jonathan, escaping from the asylum once more, took his son Richard to Darlington, working as a tanner to support them both. Still troubled, when Richard was about 11 or 12 years old, Jonathan tried to 'put him out as an assistant to a Jew hawker'.

Jonathan continued preaching, although the Wesleyan and Primitive Methodists shunned him, and he began travelling the country (he later claimed to have converted hundreds of people). By 1826, Jonathan was in Lincoln where he placed his son, Richard, in a school. Still working as a tanner, he raised enough money to have 5,000 copies of a pamphlet he had written printed, *The Life of Jonathan Martin of Darlington, tanner.* Jonathan read his manuscript to Robert Ely Leary, a young stationer, printer and bookbinder of Saint Swithin's, Lincoln, who copied it down and set it through his press. So, for the next three years, Jonathan earned his living as an itinerant tanner, hawker and fire-and-brimstone preacher. With a flair for story-telling, coupled with the many dramatic episodes of his life, Jonathan's pamphlet proved popular and gained him local notoriety. Then, at Boston in the remote Lincolnshire fenland, something of a shotgun wedding took place: Jonathan married a girl twenty years his junior, Maria Hutson:

> MARRIED. On Sunday last [19 October 1828], Jonathan Martin, journeyman tanner, of St Mary le Wigford, Lincoln, to Maria Hutson, of Bull and Magpie Lane, Boston.

Although he had known her just over four months, Maria's landlady (Jane, the wife of a shoemaker named Thomas Hindson) later remembered that he only came to her house to pay his addresses to his sweetheart for a few days before they married, by licence. Jonathan, Mrs Hindson recalled, had appeared a perfect gentleman who behaved 'exceedingly well' and, importantly as it related to future events, he had been in a sound state of mind.

Jonathan and the new Mrs Martin relocated to York and there Jonathan's mania once again manifested itself as he railed against the Church of England. He was honest about his beliefs, indeed fully owning his dispute and leaving threatening

Opposite: The Choir in York Minster, Charles Wild. (*York Museums Trust – http://yorkmuseumstrust. org.uk – Public Domain*)

notes in and around York Minster, with his initials and address (Jonathan lodged with a shoemaker at 60 Aldwark, about half a mile away from the Minster), and copies of his pamphlet were also distributed. Jonathan was 'vexed to see the idolatrous worship that was going on in the Minster, and at seeing so many bad women and men walking about … the clergy drank bottles of wine and went to play-houses.'

Matters came to a head on 1 February 1829. Jonathan visited a Methodist chapel, and then a cook's shop where he bought some soup and bread for his lunch and all the while he could hear a buzzing noise, which was caused – he claimed – by the organ playing inside the cathedral. At 4.00 pm, Jonathan slipped into the Minster for evensong, determined to stay behind when all the other worshippers had left for the evening: 'I thought that it was merely deceiving the people, that the organ made such a noise of buzz! buzz! Says I to *my sen*, "I'll have thee down tonight, thou shalt buzz no more".'

Jonathan knew what to do, for he had been shown in a dream. He cut some rope from the bell-tower and knotted it to make a ladder, utilizing his sailor's skills. Stopping to pray for guidance from the Lord, he was told to take a bible (Jonathan knew he would go to prison for what he was about to do, and thought the book would be a comfort) and a velvet curtain, all gold tassels and fringes (to 'make unto thyself a robe, like David the king, and put the fringe at the bottom of it' and the tassels on his cap). Then Jonathan set about his business, building a pile of prayer books and one of cushions. Setting fire to them both, Jonathan secured his velvet finery and bible in a bundle and, as the clock struck three, slipped out of the cathedral into the icy darkness by means of his rope ladder. Turning his face northwards, Jonathan made his way out of the city and headed to Northallerton and his brother-in-law, Joseph Carter.

Meanwhile, it took the good citizens of York a while to realize the danger; anyone out and about in the early hours kept their heads down against the chill morning air. It was not until a choirboy slipped on the ice, fell flat on his back and looked up to see the smoke rising from the cathedral that the alarm was raised. The fire brigade came post-haste and neighbouring towns sent fire engines too, but it was evening before the fire was put out. It was perhaps scant comfort at the time, but luckily most of the Minster survived and all that was lost to the fire was the choir. The finger of suspicion fell instantly on Jonathan Martin. He was captured near Hexham four days later and taken to the prison at York Castle.

The trial, on 30 March 1829, excited interest across the country. A guilty verdict would have meant death but Jonathan was declared insane and incarcerated for the rest of his days in the infamous Bedlam, otherwise Bethlem Hospital in London. There, Jonathan spent his days quietly, painting and behaving as a model patient – as long as the topic of religion was avoided – finally dying in the asylum on 27 May 1838 of a bronchial fever.

NB: The artist John Martin (1789–1854), who painted scenes of biblical disaster, and philosopher (and eccentric) William Martin (1772–1851) were Jonathan's brothers. The Scottish philosopher and writer, Thomas Carlyle, who knew the Martins, recalled that they were all 'wildish in the head!'.

The Choir of York Cathedral (after the fire in 1829), G. Nicholson. (*York Museums Trust – http:// yorkmuseumstrust.org.uk – Public Domain*)

Chapter Twenty-Five

End of an Era

We began this book at the start of the Georgian era, with the ascension of King George I, and so it is only fitting that we conclude with probably the best-known – and larger-than-life – Georgian personality: the profligate George IV, formerly the Prince of Wales and the Prince Regent.

The handsome young prince – nicknamed Prinny – lived life to the full and became a national joke, perfect fodder for the caricaturists of the day and a byword for extravagance. For George, too much was never enough. The public fell in and out of love with him but, when he died, *The Times* retrospectively said of George IV that:

> There never was an individual less regretted by his fellow low-creatures than this deceased King. What eye wept for him? What heart has heaved one throb of unmercenary sorrow?

Was this scathing opinion deserved?

George IV is certainly best remembered – even today – for his prodigious appetite, and not only his appreciation of the fare on his dinner table. The young Prince of Wales entertained many mistresses: one of the earliest was the actress Mary Robinson who, in her role as 'Perdita' to Prinny's 'Florizel', stole the prince's heart. She left the stage, only to be cast aside when the fickle prince's eye wandered further afield. After Perdita came the notorious courtesan Grace Dalrymple Elliott, who had a short-lived romance with the prince which resulted in the birth of a daughter, privately if not publicly acknowledged as the prince's progeny. Longer-lasting royal mistresses were Frances Villiers, Countess of Jersey and Elizabeth, Marchioness Conyngham, both plump, matronly women of the type George liked best.

One of George's mistresses ultimately became his morganatic and clandestine wife (in other words, no royal titles or privileges could pass to the wife or to any children of the union). Maria Anne Fitzherbert was a young Catholic widow whose 'on again, off again' relationship weathered many storms, but failed to last the course. To ease his debts, the prince officially married Caroline of Brunswick,

King George IV, Seated, in Morning Dress, Thomas Lawrence. (*Royal Pavilion & Museums, Brighton & Hove (CC BY-SA)*)

Mrs Fitzherbert, unknown artist. (*Royal Pavilion & Museums, Brighton & Hove (CC BY-SA)*)

who he hated. The union between George and Caroline was a disaster from the moment they both set eyes on one another but the prince, blind drunk, stoically managed to consummate the marriage despite his revulsion. Caroline recalled, 'he passed the greatest part of his bridal night under the grate, where he fell, and where I left him.' George later claimed that he had been intimate with Caroline only three times, twice on his wedding night and once more on the following evening. It proved to be enough: a daughter, Princess Charlotte of Wales, was born nine months later and her royal parents separated soon after. (Charlotte, George's only heir, died in childbirth in 1817 together with her infant son.)

In 1811, as a result of George III's madness, George was appointed the Prince Regent, a period in which he was highly influential and known as an arbiter of taste and style. Often accused of spending recklessly and wildly, the Prince Regent acquired works of art and fine furniture in abundance for his London residence, Carlton House (where he was advised on the furnishings by the Duchess of Devonshire and Lady Melbourne). Many pieces came from the French royal palace of Versailles; following the fall of the *Ancien Régime*, aristocratic collections were brought to London and offered for sale and the Prince Regent pragmatically bought many of the treasures that had once adorned his less fortunate rival courts. Despite criticism at the time for his wild, spendthrift ways (he was always in debt, with outstanding bills trailing in his wake), George was astute in his purchases. It is now reckoned that for every £1,000 he spent, the royal collection has gained the value of £10 million in modern money.

One of George's first acts as king was to commission the architect John Nash to transform Buckingham House into a palace. At the king's death, the transformation of Buckingham Palace was still incomplete and Nash had been dismissed due to his own costly extravagances in design (Carlton House was pulled down in the king's lifetime and the treasures within transferred to Buckingham Palace, where they remain).

Nash had previously worked with the prince on the outlandish Brighton Pavilion. Probably nothing else encapsulates George's flamboyant persona so much as this royal residence which he remodelled from a modest seafront farmhouse into a theatrical, Oriental-style pleasure dome complete with minarets.

When George eventually ascended the throne in 1820 at the age of 57, Lady Conyngham was holding the position of royal mistress. The coronation, held the following year, was a typically ostentatious affair.

The new king loved costume, theatre and pageantry. He planned an extravagant and costly spectacle, one that would never be outdone by any future monarch. Determined to outshine Napoléon Bonaparte, the man who George had viewed as his great rival and who had only recently died in exile on St Helena (when the king had been given the news that his bitterest enemy was dead, his first thought was that it was his hated wife, Caroline, and he replied: 'Is she, by God!'), George was

The Royal Pavilion at Brighton, John Nash. (*Royal Pavilion & Museums, Brighton & Hove (CC BY-SA)*)

determined that his coronation should be more spectacular than the one in which Bonaparte was crowned emperor in 1804. Ever a lover of fashion and frippery, the costumes were based on Tudor fashions and prize-fighters were hired for the day, dressed as Tudor pages, their role to deny Caroline entrance to the ceremony if she turned up (she did!). Desperate to get into the abbey, demanding to be crowned alongside her husband and crying, 'Let me pass, I am your Queen', Caroline was thwarted in her aims and retired.

Following the coronation, Lady Conyngham arranged for the king to make a visit to Ireland. However, the plans were thrown into disarray when Caroline of Brunswick died suddenly. George was conflicted by his emotions and knew that a show of false grief would be seized upon and mocked. He sailed for Ireland anyway, intending to spend the first few days of his visit in seclusion as a mark of respect. His courtiers were horrified to see him merrily disembark from the ship hours later, rolling drunk and enthusiastically shaking hands with a fisherman by the name of Pat Farrell. The Irish people loved him and he was enchanted by them.

George IV's Public Entry into the City of Dublin on August 17, 1821, Robert Havell after unknown artist. (*Yale Center for British Art, Paul Mellon Collection*)

George IV similarly won over the Scots when he paid a three-week visit to Edinburgh the next year, the first British monarch to do so for 170 years. The event was stage-managed by the author Sir Walter Scott, awash with pageantry, tartan and the sight of the king in full Highland dress, sporting a kilt over a pair of pink tights! It was a roaring success, albeit disparagingly described as 'one and twenty daft days'.

It was George's later excesses that lost him favour with the public. Increasingly overweight, often drunk and suffering from gout and cataracts among other ailments, the king relied on laudanum to dull the pain. By 1828 he was almost blind and a sorry figure, far removed from the dashing young prince of his youth. Despite his many women, the love of George IV's life remained Mrs Fitzherbert. When the king died, a diamond locket containing Maria's miniature was found around his neck.

The one thing we can say with a degree of certainty is that there will never be another Prinny!

A Voluptuary under the Horrors of Digestion, James Gillray. (*Metropolitan Museum of Art*)

Notes and Sources

e have extensively used parish registers at the relevant archives offices in our research. Contemporary newspapers, journals and other documents which we have consulted are listed below together with a selection of the books and online resources which have proved useful to our research and which we recommend as further reading.

Newspaper key: *Bath Chronicle & Weekly Gazette* (BC), *Bell's Weekly Messenger* (BW), *Brighton Gazette* (BG), *Caledonian Mercury* (CM), *Chelmsford Chronicle* (CC), *Daily Advertiser* (DA), *Derby Mercury* (DM), *Devizes & Wiltshire Gazette* (DWG),*English Chronicle,* or *Universal Evening Post* (EC), *Gazetteer & New Daily Advertiser* (GNDA), *Gazetteer & London Daily Advertiser* (GLDA), *General Evening Post* (GEP), *Hampshire Chronicle* (HC), *Ipswich Journal* (IJ), *Kentish Weekly Post,* or *Canterbury Journal* (KW), *Illustrated London News* (ILN), *Leeds Intelligencer* (LI), *Lloyd's Evening Post* (LEP), *London Courier & Evening Gazette* (LC), *London Journal* (LJ), *Manchester Courier & Lancashire General Advertiser* (MCLGA), *Morning Advertiser* (MA), *Morning Chronicle* (MC), *Morning Post & Daily Advertiser* (MP), *Newcastle Chronicle* (NCh), *Newcastle Courant* (NC), *Public Ledger & Daily Advertiser* (PL), *Reading Mercury* (RM), *Salisbury & Winchester Journal* (SWJ), *Shrewsbury Chronicle* (SC), *Stamford Mercury* (SM), *Thetford & Watton Times & People's Weekly Journal* (T&WT), *The Times* (T), *Weekly Journal* (WJ), *Weekly Packet* (WP), *Westmorland Gazette* (WG), *Whitehall Evening Post* (WEP), *World* (1787) (W), *York Herald* (YH).

Doggett's Coat and Badge
Cook, Theodore Andrea and Nickalls, Guy, *Thomas Doggett, deceased: a famous comedian* (Archibald Constable & Co., 1908)
LJ, 6 August 1720; WJ, 6 August 1715; 13 August 1720; WP, 30 July 1720; GEP, 30 July 1778

The Venus of Luxembourg
Knoll, Maria, *Letters from Liselotte: Elisabeth-Charlotte, Princess Palatine and Duchess of Orléans, 'Madame' 1652–1722* (Allison & Busby, 1998)
Saint-Simon, Louis de Rouvroy de, *An Infamous Regent's Rule, 1717–1723. An abridged translation with notes from the memoirs of the Duke de Saint-Simon*, vol. vi (New York, Brentano's, 1915–1918)

Saint-Simon, Louis de Rouvroy de, *Memoirs of Louis XIV and his court and of the regency, by the Duke of Saint-Simon*, vols. ii and iii (New York, 1910)

Soulié Eudox and Dussieux, Louis (eds), *Journal du Marquis de Dangeau avec les additions du duc de Saint-Simon* vol. 18, 1719–1720 (Paris, Firmin Didot, 1860)

The Versailles Historical Society (privately printed), *The reign and amours of the Bourbon régime; a brilliant description of the courts of Louis XIV, amours, debauchery, intrigues, and state secrets, including suppressed and confiscated Mss.; the correspondence of Madame Princess Palatine, preceded by introductions from C.-A. Saint-Beuve* (Unexpurgated rendition into English (New York, 1889))

The Velvet Coffee-Woman

Polly Peachum's Jests: In which are Comprised Most of the Witty Apothegms, Diverting Tales, and Smart Repartees that Have Been Used for Many Years Last Past, Either at St. James's Or St. Giles's: Suited Aliked to the Capacities of the Peer, and the Porter (London, 1728)

The coffee-women turn'd courtiers. An excellent new ballad (London, 1714)

Nanny Roc__d's Letter to a Member of the B__f Stake Club, in vindication of certain ladies calumniated in the Freeholder of March 9th, 1716 (London, 1716)

The Velvet Coffee-Woman: or, the Life, Gallantries and Amours of the late famous Mrs. Anne Rochford (London, 1728)

Bolard Jouslin, Claire, 'The Paradise of fools': The Freeholder (1715–1716) et l'utopie de l'opinion publique féminine en Angleterre (Université Paris 3-Sorbonne Nouvelle, Dix-huitième siècle no. 43, 2011)

Ellis, Markman, *Eighteenth-Century Coffee-House Culture*, vol. 2 (Routledge, 2017)

Crazy Sally, a Female Bonesetter

Dickson Wright, A, *Quacks Through The Ages* (Journal of the Royal Society of Arts, vol. 105, no. 4995, 1957)

IJ, 7 August 1736; 24 December 1736; NC, 14 August 1736; CM, 23 August 1736

The Polly Peerage

Coffin, Tristram Potter, *The Female Hero in Folklore and Legend* (Seabury Press, 1975)

Highfill, Philip H., Burnim, Kalan A. and Langhans, Edward A., *A Biographical Dictionary of Actors, Actresses, Musicians, Dancers, Managers & Other Stage Personnel in London, 1660–1800: Tibbett to M. West* (SIU Press, 1993)

Hilton, Lisa, *Mistress Peachum's Pleasure: The Life of Lavinia, Duchess of Bolton* (Weidenfeld & Nicolson, 2005)

London Lives: Old Bailey Proceedings: Accounts of Criminal Trials (www.londonlives.org)

Major, Joanne and Murden, Sarah, *Hannah Norsa, 18th century actress: the intricacies of relationships within her circle*, 10 Feb 2014 (www.georgianera.wordpress.com/2014/02/10/hannah-norsa-the-intricacies-of-relationships-within-her-circle)

Cecil Court on Fire
Gentleman's Magazine (1735)
Proceedings of the Old Bailey, London's Central Criminal Court, 1674 to 1913 (www.oldbaileyonline.org)
Westminster, Poor Law and Parish Administration, Examinations, City of Westminster Archives.

Jenny Cameron: The Jacobite Mystery of a Female Imposter
Chambers, Robert, *Traditions of Edinburgh*, vol. 2 (W. & C. Tait, 1825)
Fields, James Thomas, *Good Company for Every Day in the Year* (1866)
Sinclair, John, *The Statistical Account of Scotland* (1793)
Jacobite Rebellion of 1745: Jenny Cameron (www.jacobites.net)
IJ, 29 July 1749

The Queen's Ass
BC, 21 July 1763; GLDA, 13 September 1762; GNDA, 12 May 1764; LEP, 16 January 1761, 30 October 1765

Lady Wilbrahammon
Hewitt, John, *Memoirs of the celebrated Lady Viscountess Wilbrihammon, alias Mollineux, alias Irving, Countess of Normandy, and Baroness Wilmington, the greatest impostress of the present age* (Birmingham, 1778)
SWJ, 7 July 1766, 14 September 1767; NCh, 12 July 1766; LI, 26 January 1768; SC, 26 June 1773

The Queen of Smugglers
Toynbee, Mrs Paget (ed.), *The Letters of Horace Walpole, 4th Earl of Orford*, vols 5 and 7 (Clarendon Press, 1904)
Rotunda, vols 30–31 (Royal Ontario Museum, 1997)
LEP, 3 August 1764; DM, 30 December 1768; HC, 19 October 1778

Circumnavigating Sir Joseph Banks' Women
Fortescue, John (ed.), *The Correspondence of King George the Third from 1760 to December 1783, edited by Sir John Fortescue, vol.ii (1768–June 1773)* (Macmillan & Co., 1927)
Gascoigne, John, *Joseph Banks and the English Enlightenment: Useful Knowledge and Polite Culture* (Cambridge University Press, 2003)
Hamilton, James, *Gainsborough: A Portrait* (Hachette UK, 2017)
Lysaght, Averil M., *Joseph Banks in Newfoundland and Labrador, 1766: His Diary, Manuscripts, and Collections* (University of California Press, 1971)
The Town and Country Magazine; or, Universal Repository of Knowledge, Instruction, and Entertainment (September 1773)

Mrs Hartley and the 'Impudent Puppies'
Angelo, Henry, *The Reminiscences of Henry Angelo*, vol. 1 (London, 1904)

Boaden, James, *Memoirs of Mrs. Inchbald. Including her familiar correspondence with the most distinguished persons of her time* (Richard Bentley, 1833)

Cannon, John, *'Lyttelton, Thomas, second Baron Lyttelton (1744–1779)'*, Oxford Dictionary of National Biography (Oxford University Press, 2004)

Cruickshank, Dan, *The Secret History of Georgian London: How the Wages of Sin Shaped the Capital* (Random House, 2010)

Garrick, David, *The Private Correspondence of David Garrick with the most celebrated persons of his time*, vol. 1 (Richard Bentley, 1831)

Highfill, Philip H., Burnim, Kalan A. and Langhans, Edward A., *A Biographical Dictionary of Actors, Actresses, Musicians, Dancers, Managers & Other Stage Personnel in London, 1660–1800: Habgood to Houbert* (SIU Press, 1982)

The London Magazine, or, Gentleman's monthly intelligencer (October 1773)

The New Monthly magazine, vol. 51 (1837)

The Town and Country Magazine; or, Universal Repository of Knowledge, Instruction, and Entertainment (1788 supplement)

The Vauxhall affray: or, the Macaronies defeated: being a compilation of all the letters, squibs, &c. on both sides of that dispute (1773)

Emily Warren, an 'infamous and notoriously abandoned woman'

Baetjer, Katharine, *British Paintings in the Metropolitan Museum of Art, 1575–1875* (Metropolitan Museum of Art, 2009)

Bhattacharya, Sudip, *Unseen Enemy: The English, Disease, and Medicine in Colonial Bengal, 1617–1847* (Cambridge Scholars Publishing, 2014)

Cotton, William, *Sir Joshua Reynolds and His Works: Gleanings from his Diary, Unpublished Manuscripts, and from Other Sources* (Longman, 1856)

Major, Joanne and Murden, Sarah, *An Infamous Mistress: The Life, Loves and Family of the Celebrated Grace Dalrymple Elliott* (Pen & Sword, 2015)

Spencer, Alfred (ed.), *Memoirs of William Hickey, vols 1 (1749–1774), 2 (1775–1782) and 3 (1782–1790)* (Hurst & Blackett)

Bengal Past & Present, vols XXV and XXVI, Parts I and II (1923)

The Astronomer William Herschel and his Sister Caroline, a 'Heavenly Hausfrau'

Herschel, Mrs John, *Memoirs and Correspondence of Caroline Herschel* (Cambridge University Press, 1876)

Holmes, Richard, *The Age of Wonder: how the romantic generation discovered the beauty and terror of science* (HarperPress, 2009)

Winterburn, Emily, *Learned modesty and the first lady's comet: a commentary on Caroline Herschel (1787) 'An account of a new comet'* (Phil. Trans. R. Soc. A 2015 373 20140210; DOI: 10.1098/rsta.2014.0210. Published 6 March 2015)

www.datchethistory.org.uk

The Fabulously Famous Anna Maria Crouch

Devon Notes and Queries, vol. 1, Exeter (1901)

The Monthly Mirror Reflecting Men and Manners, 1795

Greig, James (ed.), *The Farington Diary [1793–1821]: July 13, 1793 to August 24, 1802*, vol. 1 (London, 1922)

Kelly, Michael, *Reminiscences of Michael Kelly, of the King's Theatre, and Theatre Royal Drury Lane, including a period of nearly half a century; with original anecdotes of many distinguished persons, political, literary and musical* (1826)

Young, Mary Julia, *Memoirs of Mrs Crouch: Including Retrospect of the Stage* (London, 1806)

MP, 11 November 1780, 12 January 1785; GNDA, 13 November 1780; WEP, 20 September 1783, 28 May 1785; KW, 4 November 1794; BG, 25 November 1908

The will of Rawlins Edward or Rawlings Calvert, late Crouch, Cornwall Record Office, CRO ref SO/W/327

Up, Up and Away

Davies, Mark, *King of All Balloons: The Adventurous Life of James Sadler, the First English Aeronaut* (Amberley Publishing Limited, 2015)

Highfill, Philip H., Burnim, Kalan A. and Langhans, Edward A., *A Biographical Dictionary of Actors, Actresses, Musicians, Dancers, Managers, and Other Stage Personnel in London, 1660–1800: S. Siddons to Thynne* (SIU Press, 1991)

Jennings, Humphrey, *Pandaemonium 1660–1886: The Coming of the Machine as Seen by Contemporary Observers* (Icon Books Ltd, 2012)

Kotar, S.L. and Gessler, J.E., *Ballooning: A History, 1782–1900* (McFarland, 2010)

Major, Joanne and Murden, Sarah, *An Infamous Mistress: The Life, Loves and Family of the Celebrated Grace Dalrymple Elliott* (Pen & Sword, 2015)

Toynbee, Mrs Paget (ed.), *The Letters of Horace Walpole, 4th Earl of Orford* (Clarendon Press, 1905)

The European magazine, and London review; containing the literature, history, politics, arts, manners and amusements of the age (1782–1826)

The Town and Country Magazine; or, Universal Repository of Knowledge, Instruction, and Entertainment (May 1785)

LC, 30 November 1784; CC, 6 May 1785; RM, 4 July 1785

French Revolution: The Flight to Varennes

Major, Joanne and Murden, Sarah, *An Infamous Mistress: The Life, Loves and Family of the Celebrated Grace Dalrymple Elliott* (Pen & Sword, 2015)

Brighton's Travelling Windmill

Dawes, H.T., *The Windmills and Millers of Brighton*, 2nd edition (Sussex Mills Group, 2002)

KW, 7 April 1797; HC, 29 October 1821

To Kill the King: Frith the Madman

Major, Joanne and Murden, Sarah, *Margaret Nicholson: the woman who attempted to assassinate King George III*, 2 August 2014 (www.georgianera.wordpress.com/2014/08/02/margaret-nicholson-the-woman-who-attempted-to-assassinate-king-george-iii)

DA, 12 October 1772; EC, 23 January 1790; GEP, 2 March 1790; W, 22 January 1790

The Norfolk Nymph: A Female Jockey
Calumny combated. A complete vindication of Col. Thornton's conduct in his transactions with Mr. Burton, second edition (1806)
Pierce Egan's book of sports, and mirror of life: embracing the turf, the chase, the ring, and the stage: interspersed with original memoirs of sporting men, etc. (W. Tegg & Co., 1847)
Thormanby, *Kings of the Rod, Rifle and Gun*, vol. 1 (Hutchinson & Co., 1901)
LC, 27 August 1804; BW, 9 September 1804; MP, 11 September 1804, 2 April 1806; PL, 27 August 1805; YH, 5 April 1806; TWT, 18 September 1886

Martha Udny, aka 'Mrs Nibs'
Holme, Thea, *Prinny's daughter: a life of Princess Charlotte of Wales* (Hamilton, 1976)
Williams, Kate, *Becoming Queen* (Arrow Books, 2009)

King of the Resurrection Men
Millard, Ann, *An account of the circumstances attending the imprisonment and death of the late William Millard, formerly superintendent of the Theatre of Anatomy of St. Thomas's Hospital, Southwark* (1825)
MC, 17 July 1823; MP, 25 August 1823; MA, 16 October 1823

Caroline Crachami: The Sicilian Fairy
Dobson, Jessie, *The story of Caroline Crachami, the Sicilian Dwarf* (1955)
Smythies, Captain R.H. Raymond, *Historical Records of the 40th (2nd Somersetshire) Regiment* (1894)
Wood, Gaby, *The Smallest of all Persons Mentioned in the Records of Littleness* (Profile Books, 1998)
The National Archives:
   British Army Muster Books and Pay Lists 1812–1817
   Royal Hospital Chelsea: Admission Books, Registers and Papers 1702–1876 and Regimental Registers of Pensions, 1713–1882
   Royal Hospital Kilmainham Pensioner Discharge Documents 1724–1924
The Annual Register, Or, A View of the History, Politics and Literature of the Year (1824)
DWG, 22 April 1824; MP, 10 June 1824; LC, 16 June 1824; ILN, 4 October 1845; MC, 8 July 1848

The Dramatic Life of Jonathan Martin, tanner
Campbell, Ian, Christianson, Aileen and McIntosh, Sheila (eds), *The collected letters of Thomas and Jane Welsh Carlyle*, vol.17 (Duke University Press, 1990)
Martin, Jonathan, *The Life of Jonathan Martin of Darlington, tanner, written by himself* (1826)
Report of the Trial of Jonathan Martin, for having, on the night of the first of February, 1829, set fire to York Minster (1829)
Bethlem Hospital patient admission registers and casebooks, 1683–1932
SM, 24 October 1828

End of an Era

Major, Joanne and Murden, Sarah, *A Right Royal Scandal: Two Marriages That Changed History* (Pen & Sword, 2016)

Major, Joanne and Murden, Sarah, *'One and twenty daft days' in 1822: King George IV visits Scotland, Joanne Major and Sarah Murden*, 4 August 2015 (www.georgianera. wordpress.com/2015/08/04/one-and-twenty-daft-days-in-1822-king-george-iv-visits-scotland)

Art, Passion & Power: The Story of the Royal Collection. Episode 3, 'Palaces and Pleasure domes' (BBC 4). Directed by Sebastian Barfield; presented by Andrew Graham-Dixon; 2018

WG, 10 July 1830; T, 30 December 1900

Also by the Same Authors

An Infamous Mistress: The Life, Loves and Family of the Celebrated Grace Dalrymple Elliott **(Pen & Sword, 2015)**

Divorced wife, infamous mistress, prisoner in France during the French Revolution and the reputed mother of the Prince of Wales's child, notorious eighteenth-century courtesan Grace Dalrymple Elliott lived an amazing life in eighteenth- and early nineteenth-century London and Paris.

Strikingly tall and beautiful, later lampooned as 'Dally the Tall' in newspaper gossip columns, she left her Scottish roots and convent education behind to reinvent herself in a 'marriage à-la-mode', but before she was even legally an adult she was cast off and forced to survive on just her beauty and wits.

The authors of this engaging and, at times, scandalous book intersperse the story of Grace's tumultuous life with anecdotes of her fascinating family, from those who knew Thomas Jefferson and George Washington and who helped to abolish slavery, to those who were, like Grace, mistresses of great men.

While this book is the most definitive biography of Grace Dalrymple Elliott ever written, it is much more than that; it is Grace's family history that traces her ancestors from their origin in the Scottish borders, to their move south to London. It follows them to France, America, India, Africa and elsewhere, offering a broad insight into the social history of the Georgian era, comprising the ups and downs, the highs and lows of life at that time.

This is the remarkable and detailed story of Grace set, for the first time, in the context of her wider family and told more completely than ever before.

Reviews:

Courtesan. Spy. Survivor. A gripping and meticulously-researched account of the swashbuckling life of one of history's most overlooked heroines. – Hallie Rubenhold, author of *The Scandalous Lady W.*

An Infamous Mistress is a fascinating read, yet it's more than that. If anything, it's a shining example of research done well, presented coherently on the perfect subject: a powerful courtesan that time forgot. – *History of Royals* magazine, May 2016.

***A Right Royal Scandal: Two Marriages That Changed History* (Pen & Sword, 2016)**

Almost two books in one, *A Right Royal Scandal* recounts the fascinating history of the irregular love matches contracted by two successive generations of the Cavendish-Bentinck family, ancestors of the British Royal Family. The first part of this intriguing book looks at the scandal that erupted in Regency London, just months after the Battle of Waterloo, when the widowed Lord Charles Bentinck eloped with the Duke of Wellington's married niece. A messy divorce and a swift marriage followed, complicated by an unseemly tug-of-war over Lord Charles' infant daughter from his first union. Over two decades later and while at Oxford University, Lord Charles' eldest son, known to his family as Charley, fell in love with a beautiful gypsy girl and secretly married her. He kept this union hidden from his family, in particular his uncle, William Henry Cavendish-Scott-Bentinck, 4th Duke of Portland, upon whose patronage he relied. When his alliance was discovered, Charley was cast adrift by his family, with devastating consequences.

A love story as well as a brilliantly-researched historical biography, this is a continuation of Joanne and Sarah's first biography, *An Infamous Mistress*, about the eighteenth-century courtesan Grace Dalrymple Elliott, whose daughter was the first wife of Lord Charles Bentinck. The book ends by showing how, if not for a young gypsy and her tragic life, the British monarchy would look very different today.

Reviews:

Major and Murden keep their text entertaining and light throughout, making for an easy read of a subject that keeps you engrossed from start to finish. This book is brilliant for those who enjoy the scandals of historical television, with the added authenticity of historical fact. – *History of Royals* magazine, February 2017.

This excellent, heartfelt and touching read is highly recommended for anyone with an interest in the nineteenth-century British aristocracy. – Dr Jacqueline Reiter, author of *The Late Lord: The Life of John Pitt – 2nd Earl of Chatham*.

A Georgian Heroine: The Intriguing Life of Rachel Charlotte Williams Biggs (Pen & Sword, 2017)

Rachel Charlotte Williams Biggs lived an incredible life, one which proved that fact is often much stranger than fiction. As a young woman she endured a tortured existence at the hands of a male tormentor, but emerged from that to reinvent herself as a playwright and author; a political pamphleteer and a spy, working for the British government and later single-handedly organizing George III's jubilee celebrations. Trapped in France during the revolutionary years of 1792–95, she published an anonymous account of her adventures. However, was everything as it seemed? The extraordinary Mrs Biggs lived life on her own terms in an age when it was a man's world, using politicians as her mouthpiece in the Houses of Parliament and corresponding with the greatest men of the day. Throughout it all though, she held on to the ideal of her one youthful true love, a man who abandoned her to her fate and spent his entire adult life in India. Who was this amazing lady?

In *A Georgian Heroine: The Intriguing Life of Rachel Charlotte Williams Biggs*, we delve into her life to reveal her accomplishments and lay bare Mrs Biggs' continued reinvention of herself. This is the bizarre but true story of an astounding woman persevering in a man's world.

Reviews:

I could not recommend a more delightful heroine to you than Charlotte. The authors have done a thoroughly-researched job of bringing her story to light in a fast-paced narrative. I recommend it! – Regan Walker, award-winning and best-selling author of historical romance.

A remarkable story, beautifully told. – *Books Monthly*.